Scorpio
24 October – 22 November

DID YOU PURCHASE THIS BOOK WITHOUT A COVER?
If you did, you should be aware it is **stolen property** as it was
reported *unsold and destroyed* by a retailer. Neither the author nor
the publisher has received any payment for this book.

*All Rights Reserved including the right of reproduction in whole or
in part in any form. This edition is published by arrangement with
Harlequin Enterprises II B.V./S.à.r.l. The text of this publication or
any part thereof may not be reproduced or transmitted in any form
or by any means, electronic or mechanical, including photocopying,
recording, storage in an information retrieval system, or otherwise,
without the written permission of the publisher.*

*This book is sold subject to the condition that it shall not, by way of
trade or otherwise, be lent, resold, hired out or otherwise circulated
without the prior consent of the publisher in any form of binding or
cover other than that in which it is published, and without a similar
condition including this condition being imposed on the subsequent
purchaser.*

® *and* ™ *are trademarks owned and used by the trademark owner
and/or its licensee. Trademarks marked with* ® *are registered with the
United Kingdom Patent Office and/or the Office for Harmonisation
in the Internal Market and in other countries.*

*First published in Great Britain 2008
by Harlequin Mills & Boon Limited,
Eton House, 18-24 Paradise Road, Richmond, Surrey TW9 1SR*

Copyright © Dadhichi Toth 2007, 2008 & 2009

ISBN: 978 0 263 86911 8

Typeset at Midland Typesetters Australia

*Harlequin Mills & Boon policy is to use papers that are
natural, renewable and recyclable products and made from
wood grown in sustainable forests. The logging and
manufacturing processes conform to the legal environmental
regulations of the country of origin.*

*Printed and bound in Spain
by Litografia Rosés S.A., Barcelona*

About Dadhichi

Dadhichi is one of Australia's foremost astrologers, and is frequently seen on TV and in the media. He has the unique ability to draw from complex astrological theory to provide clear, easily understandable advice and insights for people who want to know what their future may hold.

In the 25 years that Dadhichi has been practising astrology, and conducting face and other esoteric readings, he has provided over 9,000 consultations. His clients include celebrities, political and diplomatic figures and media and corporate identities from all over the world.

Dadhichi's unique blend of astrology and face reading helps people fulfil their true potential. His extensive experience practising western astrology is complemented by his research into the theory and practice of eastern forms of astrology.

Dadhichi has been a guest on many Australian television shows and several of his political and worldwide forecasts have proved uncannily accurate. He has appeared on many of Australia's leading television networks and is a regular columnist for several Australian magazines.

His websites www.astrology.com.au, www.facereader.com and soulmate.com.au which attract hundreds of thousands of visitors each month, offer a wide variety of features, helpful information and services.

Dedicated to The Light of Intuition
Sri V. Krishnaswamy—mentor and friend

With thanks to Julie, Joram, Isaac and Janelle

Welcome from Dadhichi

Dear Friend,

It's a pleasure knowing you're reading this, your astrological forecast for 2009. There's nothing more exciting than looking forward to a bright new year and considering what the stars have in store and how you might make the most of what's on offer in your life.

Apart from the anticipation of what I might predict will happen to you, of what I say about your upcoming luck and good fortune, remember that astrology is first and foremost a tool of personal growth, self-awareness and inner transformation. What 'happens to us' is truly a reflection of what we're giving out; the signals we are transmitting to our world, our universe.

The astrological adage of 'As above, so below' can also be interpreted in a slightly different way when I say 'As within, so without'! In other words, as hard as it is to believe, the world and our experiences of it, or our relationships and circumstances, good or bad, do tend to mirror our own belief systems and mental patterns.

It is for this reason that I thought I'd write a brief introductory note to remind you that the stars are pointers to your wonderful destiny and that you must work with them to realise your highest and most noble goals. The greatest marvel and secret is your own inner self! Astrology reveals these inner secrets of your character, which are the foundation of your life's true purpose.

What is about to happen to you this year is exciting, but what you *do* with this special power of knowledge, how you share your talents with others, and the way you truly enjoy each moment of your life is far more important than knowing *what* will happen. This is the key to a 'superior' kind of happiness. It will start to open up to you when you live in harmony with your true nature as shown by astrology.

I really hope you enjoy your coming twelve months, and gain new insights and fresh perspectives on your life through studying your 2009 horoscope. Here's hoping great success will be yours and health, love and happiness will follow wherever you go.

I leave you now with the words of a wise man, who once said:

> Sow a thought, and you reap an act;
> Sow an act, and you reap a habit;
> Sow a habit, and you reap a character;
> Sow a character, and you reap a destiny.
> Your thoughts are the architects of your destiny.

Warm regards, and may the stars shine brightly for you in 2009!

Your Astrologer,

Dadhichi Toth

Contents

The Scorpio Identity 9

Scorpio: A Snapshot 10

Star Sign Compatibility 27

2009: The Year Ahead 51

2009: Month By Month Predictions 61

January 62

February 66

March 70

April 74

May 78

June 82

July 86

August 90

September 94

October 98

November 102

December 106

2009: Astronumerology 111

2009: Your Daily Planner 133

The Scorpio Identity

Welcome anything that comes to you, but do not long for anything else.

—Andride

Scorpio: A Snapshot

Key characteristics

Secretive, passionate, determined, tactless, loyal, hardworking and inflexible

Compatible star signs

Scorpio, Taurus, Capricorn, Cancer, Pisces

Key life phrase

I will

Life goals

To transform yourself into the best you can become

Platinum assets

Ability to overcome at all costs, sexual attractiveness and will power

Zodiac totem

The scorpion, the lizard, the phoenix

Zodiac symbol

♏

Zodiac facts

Eighth sign of the zodiac; fixed, fertile, feminine, moist

THE SCORPIO IDENTITY

Element

Water

Famous Scorpios

Hillary Rodham Clinton, Bill Gates, Joaquin Phoenix, Bjork, Julia Roberts, Richard Dreyfuss, Winona Ryder, Indira Gandhi, Carl Sagan, Joni Mitchell, Demi Moore, Leonardo DiCaprio, Larry Flynt, Prince Charles of Windsor, Bill Bryson, Martin Scorsese, Boris Becker, Calvin Klein, Jodie Foster, Bill Wyman, k.d. lang and Pablo Picasso

Key to karma, spirituality and emotional balance

Your keywords are 'I will' and your biggest challenge is to let go of your need to control others. In your last life the sign of Cancer dominated your existence and because of this you are strongly drawn to the idea of family, nurturing and selfless love. Try to use some of these qualities to unconditionally share your feelings with others.

Spend at least a little time in meditation, especially on Mondays, Tuesdays and Sundays, as this will bring you inner peace and tranquillity.

Scorpio: Your profile

It's not easy being a Scorpio, especially when you find yourself confronted by others asking, 'What star sign are you?' and then having to almost mutter it under your breath for fear they are going to run away, or somehow become defensive the moment you mention you happen to be ... yes ... a Scorpio!

Scorpio certainly has been misunderstood and it is unfortunate, because not all crazy people are born under that sign! Nonetheless, a bad reputation has developed over many hundreds of years and you'll often find yourself disproving this once others get to know you a little better.

SCORPIO

You were born when the Sun was moving through the eighth sign of the zodiac, that is, Scorpio, which refers to the most hidden, secretive and complex part of the heavens. Is it any wonder you have such a deep and intricate personality?

People do find it hard to understand you but once they get a taste for your Scorpio character they realise that your passion for life (not just sex, mind you) is absolutely second to none. You are committed to everything you do and this ranges from the work you perform to the relationships you choose. There are no half-measures for you and, in being so demanding of yourself and others, eventually you realise that not everyone can deal with you as easily as you would expect.

You live hard, you live fast, and life for you is a challenge. You believe in Darwin's law of survival of the fittest. Often you lack the sensitivity to realise that not everyone is a leader or conqueror and that, in fact, most are followers. You'll need to be more accommodating of others on your life journey.

You push yourself to the limits in every department of life and constantly need to feel as if you are achieving something. This is probably why, as I said earlier, people are taken aback when you say you are a Scorpio. You truly are an exemplary figure in that you give 100 per cent of yourself to whatever you believe in. You demand the same of others.

One historic fact about Scorpio isn't at all untrue, and that relates to your sexual and magnetic quality. Scorpio is the sexual sign of the zodiac and you flaunt this wherever you go. Whether you are a male or female you know you possess an intangible quality that tends to attract anyone and everyone to you. Often, little do they know that this is very much like a moth being drawn to the flame. You know exactly how to entice others to do your bidding.

Your magnetic power is your greatest strength and you convey this through your eyes. People often comment on just how deep and bewitching your eyes are. You certainly know

THE SCORPIO IDENTITY

how to express your thoughts through them, which is why you don't necessarily have to speak to communicate. Others will always know what you are feeling simply by a look or, God forbid, a stare. If you are unhappy or angry, those laser eyes of yours can 'kill'.

You have no fear of the obstacles in life, believing that this is what strengthens a person and helps them transform into something newer and better. You are a formidable competitor because of this strength and you thrive on challenges. There aren't too many occasions when you don't win. You're obsessive in everything you do, ,especially in love, so this often makes you possessive and jealous. This is one trait you need to work on improving if you are to enjoy your relationships more fully.

Some people see you as a ruthless character, someone who is not easily satisfied no matter how hard they try. Some of the tougher Scorpio-born individuals are even vengeful and destructive if others don't live up to their expectations, or happen to cross them. I hope you have these destructive qualities under control.

You have the desire to help others and your successes are shared around with friends and family because you like them to be part of your journey and to be well looked after.

Many Scorpios reach the top of the tree in life and are one of a rare breed that never gives in. You probably know what I mean by that because you have the power of endurance, patience and intuitive power that allows you to achieve your goals through thick or thin.

Scorpio is also rare in that it has three totems that rule it— the scorpion, the grey lizard and the phoenix. The scorpion represents the lower and destructive aspects of your star sign. The grey lizard affects those types who are inwardly reclusive and not yet developed, whereas the phoenix fully represents the self-actualised scorpion who rises to the pinnacle of human achievement.

SCORPIO

Three classes of Scorpio

If you were born between the 24th of October and the 2nd of November you are an intensely sensual character but you do have noble aspirations. Pleasure will be a focal point for you and in your earlier life you may spend a lot of time exploring the sexual part of your personality.

Being born between the 3rd and the 11th of November makes you more idealistic and spiritual by nature. You have a strong leaning towards understanding the meaning of life and delving deeply into the true nature of your being.

If you were born between the 12th and the 22nd of November you are one of the more sensitive types of Scorpio because you have strong lunar vibrations. Your challenge will be to bring your emotions under control and not be swayed by the events of life. You have a very caring and family oriented nature as well.

Scorpio role model: Hillary Clinton

Hillary Clinton was first known as the wife of ex-president Bill Clinton. From there she became dedicated towards making a name for herself as a politician and has even committed to becoming the first female president of the United States. As a Scorpio we see in her those traits of determination, passion and principle, which mark her out among others. It's rare for a Scorpio like Hillary not to succeed.

Scorpio: The light side

You are one of the most magnetic people among us and you can use this power to create an immense amount of good in the world. You inspire others with your extraordinary achievements, which are centred on your determination to win at all costs. Any number of obstacles will never deter you from your goal once you have made up your mind.

THE SCORPIO IDENTITY

You have great seductive skills and are the expert sensualist in the zodiac. You know how to love—not just physically but also emotionally, mentally and spiritually. For you love is a total experience and with the right person you know how to love totally.

You are dependable and are able to show others the proper way to work and produce great results. The more evolved Scorpio is a humanitarian as well but doesn't always boast about this. Scorpios often use silence as a great source of power and this usually helps them achieve their ends.

Because Scorpio is transformative by nature, you are a healer. You are able to generate healing power through your hands; but your mere presence also is able to bring things under control and help others feel much better. You are intuitive by nature and have the ability to solve problems through relying on your psychic hunches.

Scorpio: The shadow side

Because you have power over others, you must learn to use this with great discrimination and never manipulate people for your own selfish ends. You coerce others against their will and once you decide on a course of action, can be inflexible in gaining what you want, irrespective of other people's feelings in the matter. Try to be inclusive of others as well as they often have a part to play in your success and you should acknowledge that.

If someone crosses you in some way you can be ruthlessly unforgiving and vengeful. Not only do you cut them off—this is not enough for you—you must inflict maximum damage to make the point that you will not be undermined again. It's also important that you learn to let go of things graciously. Some Scorpios hold grudges for years until they have had the chance for payback. Please, don't be like this.

Sexuality can become excessive and obsessive with some Scorpios who want to push themselves to the limits. If you

SCORPIO

don't manage this aspect of yourself it may become a source of problems in developing a deeper and more intimate relationship with the one you love.

You are a loyal individual but demand an extra dose of return loyalty from those you cherish. Smothering them with your love and trying to possess them is not the way to draw them closer. Let go a little more, relax and enjoy your love life.

Scorpio woman

Scorpio is a feminine sign so the Scorpio woman naturally projects this quality in her life and people notice her for this very reason.

Yes, you are a Scorpio woman and this seductive, feminine trait is yours and shines through everything you do. However, your typical type of femininity is not dainty, soft and submissive. You are quite the opposite and have an edge that makes you both magnetically attractive and dangerous at the same time.

You are able to lure people with your quick wit and clever humour and in a surprise attack later reveal the deeper, multifaceted aspects of your personality. You are indeed a chameleon character and only the most advanced soul will understand you.

You have no respect for weakness and your friends realise they have to make an extra effort to lift their game to match your own power if they're going to continue to be a friend. You are an all or nothing girl. These same principles apply as much, if not more, to the realm of relationships. Your Scorpio intensity will blow apart the average suitor and so only the most resilient and special type of man is suited to you. To others you seem black and white but this again is part of your smoke and mirrors tactic to weed out the men from the boys.

You have an unusual approach in that you are quite possessive of your partner but demand freedom for yourself. In

THE SCORPIO IDENTITY

this sense you can be contradictory and send out confusing signals. If you demand this sort of loyalty from others you must give it back. I am pleased to say that the Scorpio woman does, and that the sense of freedom she seeks is not a deceptive type of freedom, but one in which she can explore her inner self to the utmost level.

Immense confidence is part of your personality and this coupled with your sense of humour makes you set for success in any area you choose. Your confidence is sometimes disarming to others, as you appear arrogant in style. You're quick, sharp and straight to the point and unfortunately others misinterpret your motives because of this. Try to adapt yourself to the different characters you engage with and this won't be so much of a problem for you.

Another contradictory signal you give off is related to your wonderful sexual energy. If men think you are using this to gain an advantage professionally or socially, they are very much mistaken. It is an assumption they sometimes make with a Scorpio woman, but how wrong they are! Here again is another inconsistency that will forever keep the pundits puzzling over your character. Yes, the Scorpio woman is a perplexing creation of God.

You will always use your intuition to decide whether others are being honest with you or not. You are a great judge of character and many Scorpio women are drawn into the esoteric arts displaying great natural ability for tarot, astrology and clairvoyance. Apart from any professional use of this power, it will always hold you in good stead and you should trust these inner promptings before making any decision in life.

You are outspoken and never afraid to call a spade a spade. You tell people what you think of their opinions *and* them. Not everyone will always like you but they will always know where they stand with you. You create enemies as well as

SCORPIO

friends but would far prefer to be seen as an honest individual and this is just the way it is for a Scorpio woman.

Scorpio women make excellent mothers and protect and nourish their young with huge amounts of love, affection and dedication. You are uncompromising and resourceful and this too is another one of your greatest assets in life.

Scorpio man

Scorpio men are both emotionally and physically passionate. You only have to look deep into their eyes to see their intensity of purpose. Their depth and passion is visible yet quite unnerving.

The Scorpio male often doesn't like to admit that he has a high level of intuition and psychic power as he knows that it is fully developed within him. If you were born under this sign you can stop pretending and start using this to benefit the world and yourself.

You appear to have a big ego but that is your protective mechanism helping you get through life. Many Scorpio men undergo rather difficult childhoods in which they have to toughen up early and this, although at first it appears to be a limitation, becomes one of their greatest strengths.

You've learned the art of persistence, determination and follow through. Although Scorpio is not considered a flexible personality type because of the fixity of this Sun sign, you are indeed adaptable if that is required of you. Generally, however, you call the shots and others need to take the orders.

Addictions can sometimes be a problem for Scorpios, so take your pick: sex, money, power, or perhaps all three? Many Scorpios become workaholics because they have to perfect their work and become the best in their game. Sexually you will explore all aspects to your satisfaction and this is a good idea so that you can eventually settle down and bring to the fore the loving, nurturing and compassionate aspects of your water sign.

There are times when you seem disconnected from others and this is not in any way a reflection on them, but rather your own self-absorption in an idea and a cause. You can be dismissive of them and, although you are not aware of the impact it has on them, it can be quite insulting. Try to be more sensitive to how people perceive you and your relationships will definitely be all the better for it. Silence is another one of your most notable characteristics.

You generate a lot of energy, power and control through this one technique. It gives you leverage in business but can make you seem hard and uncommunicative in your personal relationships. If you must use the silent treatment on others, it's not a bad idea to use it judiciously so as not to alienate others. The world will reflect who you are in their responses to you. Remember that.

Scorpio child

The water signs are the most evolved of the zodiac circle and Scorpio is no exception. Children born under this sign are therefore souls who have been around the cosmic block a few times. You'll get a hint of that when you look into their eyes and feel an old man or woman is looking back at you from within.

The young Scorpio child has a retentive memory and is able to retain any sort of information you feed him or her. Along with their intuitive senses, they can spot a fraud a mile away, so don't try to pull the wool over their eyes because they are way too quick for you. This can be a little uncomfortable, especially if you're trying to think up excuses to get away for the night or simply have some time out. The child of Scorpio knows exactly what you are up to and you'll have to do better than that.

SCORPIO

Scorpio children are resilient. They are able to handle much more than other kids, which is why they become tough competitors as they get older. They certainly are sensitive and aware but are sufficiently thick-skinned enough to cope with the challenges of life.

Your Scorpio child is competitive and needs proper outlets to shine in sports or other academic fields. Give them the love and support they need to make this happen. Because Scorpio children are so loyal, they make popular friends but also need to be the centre of attention. They can often be domineering so it's best to teach them the rules of engagement and that give and take is part of the social structure of our society. They'll learn soon enough and will become even more popular.

Scorpio children are explorers both of the outer world and their inner selves. Being curious and adventurous they want to find the answers to all their questions and so you'll be constantly trying to dig up information to satisfy their curiosity.

Scorpio teenage years are sometimes difficult because they are attracted to the dark side as much as the light, so they need the value of good company that will help them grow into well-adjusted adults.

Because Scorpio is secretive, try to respect your child's need for their own private space and being alone. Within this safe haven they will grow emotionally and spiritually.

Romance, love and marriage

As a native of Scorpio you are probably well aware of your sexuality, even well before puberty, but may not have understood what this was. You have a sense of boy–girl relationships because sexuality, sensuality and transformation are the key words of your star sign.

Once you arrived at puberty and discovered the meaning of this energy, it was as if a torrential flood of passion, love, lust

THE SCORPIO IDENTITY

and intensity had been unleashed. I only hope you've learned to direct this energy well because you are by far the most complex lover of the zodiac.

Scorpios can either be sensually intimate or cold and unapproachable. It's important for you to use sexuality as the transformative power to help you grow spiritually. You have an instinctive urge to explore this part of life and nature.

You like to keep matters of sex, love and relationships secretive. But, with the person you love you can be extremely demonstrative and affectionate. You need someone who can match the intensity of your love and overt nature. You're extreme once you give your heart to someone and the one thing you detest more than anything is being with someone who is insipid, half-hearted and shallow. You can't understand how others can't feel the depths of love as you do. You must understand that you are in a unique position and that you are the exception rather than the rule.

Due to this, you may not always find it easy in your search for that special soulmate. You have to exercise patience and will probably have to go through many relationships until the first one of this special calibre comes your way. Scorpio is not only faithful but is prepared to die for their love. This again reflects the depth and intensity of your passion.

Once the opportunity to engage yourself in a meaningful relationship presents itself, you become extremely attached to that person. They become the object of worship and most of your activities become centred on them. You want to love them, nourish them, support them and you may even want to direct their lives. This can be the beginning of problems for you because your love can sometimes be seen as irrational and overwhelming. Be gentle and move slowly once you meet your soulmate. Don't rush things. Slowly bring them around to your way of love.

There is an extreme side to your nature that is exhibited when you feel moody or a little depressed. You can withdraw

SCORPIO

like a tortoise withdrawing into its shell. When you're angry or disappointed with someone, your means of punishing them is your silence. A wall of ice is how some would describe your tactics of disengaging in this situation. You must learn to speak about how you feel, especially if you're upset, as this will not only lessen your internal burden but also foster a better communication with your friend, spouse or lover.

The signs of Cancer, Pisces, Virgo and Capricorn are the better signs of compatibility and these individuals will understand your varied and sometimes difficult ways. Your opposite star sign Taurus will act as a balance in many areas but may at times be just as inflexible as yourself. You will feel satisfied in relationships with any of the people born under these star signs.

Scorpio men and women make some of the best homemakers and family life is important to them. You and your partner will spend a lot of time creating and nurturing each other and your children. Scorpio is naturally inclined to protect the people they love. There are few star signs that possess as much tenacity as you in doing whatever it takes to provide a safe haven for your family. Against great odds you will create a wonderful home life for those under your care.

Overall Scorpio has a strong principle-based approach to love and relationships and, if you're able to manage some of the deeper and extreme sides of your personality, you should be able to enjoy a fulfilling life of love and passion for many years to come.

Health, wellbeing and diet

Because Scorpio is a particularly deep and emotional sign, it is important for you to find balance in this aspect of your personality. Many of your health issues will stem primarily from the area of your emotionalism.

Scorpio generally rules the reproductive, sexual and excretory systems of the body and, if your emotions are not

THE SCORPIO IDENTITY

functioning well, or you don't drink enough water, it could be that these areas may be prone to problems as you get older.

Work is also important to you; but as I mentioned earlier, many Scorpios have a tendency to work long hours without listening to their body's signals for adequate rest. Sleep—at least seven or eight hours a night—will replenish your energy reserves and overcome a predisposition to disease because of this.

Adequate sport is also important for you to let off steam and to work through some of your competitive and emotional urges. For the most part Scorpio has an immense willpower that allows them to overcome health problems and to enjoy high vitality, good health and long life.

Water signs tend to overeat so you must moderate your intake of calories and eat smaller meals, not mixing too many different types of food. You're always on the go so another important point is to take time to sit down and really eat your food, chewing it and enjoying it while you do so.

Hot and fiery Mars as well as Pluto rule Scorpio. Spicy foods, chilli and curry dishes are a favourite of many of you but this can be irritating so again moderation is the key word to enjoying your rich and sumptuous feasts without adversely affecting your health.

The orange and red vegetables such as pumpkin, beetroot or sweet potato are excellent sources of nutrition for you, Scorpio. Red beans and lentils also offer you the additional high protein that you require for your long bouts of work or sport. Eat smaller meals and most importantly you shouldn't eat when emotionally upset or angry with someone.

Work

With the Sun ruling your professional life, you need to shine and be the best at what you do. It doesn't matter much

SCORPIO

whether you are an employer or employee because hard work, perseverance and strong ambitions are deeply ingrained into your Scorpio mentality. You are self-motivated and achieve what you set out to do.

Scorpio is a transformative sign and therefore anything you attempt needs to reflect this quality. Great surgeons, psychologists and psychiatrists are born under the sign of Scorpio. Metaphysical healing falls under this category because you have intuitive power and healing energies in your hands as well.

Because of your detective-like nature, you are a problem solver and can make a good researcher, detective or policeman. Other suitable professions include being in the armed forces, an astrologer, psychic adviser, or in banking and investment fields.

Because Jupiter has a strong influence over your finances and your investments, you might do well in the stock market or other fields in which you need to take some sort of gamble.

For the most part a Scorpio career is a successful one and one in which money, fame and inner personal satisfaction are not uncommon for those born under this sign.

Your lucky days

Your luckiest days are Mondays, Tuesdays, Thursdays and Sundays.

Your lucky numbers

Remember that the forecasts given later in the book will help you optimise your chances of winning. Your lucky numbers are:

9, 18, 27, 36, 45, 54

3, 12, 21, 30, 48, 57

2, 11, 20, 29, 38, 47, 56

THE SCORPIO IDENTITY

Your destiny years

Your most important years are 9, 18, 27, 36, 45, 54, 63, 72 and 81.

SCORPIO

Star Sign Compatibility

A kiss makes the heart young again and wipes out the years.

—Rupert Brooke

Romantic compatibility

How compatible are you with your current partner, lover or friend? Did you know that astrology can reveal a whole new level of understanding between people simply by looking at their star sign and that of their partner? In this chapter I'd like to share some special insights that will help you better appreciate your strengths and challenges using Sun sign compatibility.

The Sun reflects your drive, willpower and personality. The essential qualities of two star signs blend like two pure colours producing an entirely new colour. Relationships, similarly, produce their own emotional colours when two people interact. The following is a general guide to your romantic prospects with others and how, by knowing the astrological 'colour' of each other, the art of love can help you create a masterpiece.

When reading the following I ask you to remember that no two star signs are ever *totally* incompatible. With effort and compromise, even the most 'difficult' astrological matches can work. Don't close your mind to the full range of life's possibilities! Learning about each other and ourselves is the most important facet of astrology.

Each star sign combination is followed by the elements of those star signs and the result of their combining. For instance, Aries is a fire sign and Aquarius is an air sign, and this combination produces a lot of 'hot air'. Air feeds fire, and fire warms air. In fact, fire requires air. However, not all air and fire combinations work. I have included information about the different birth periods within each star sign and this will throw even more light on your prospects for a fulfilling love life with any star sign you choose.

STAR SIGN COMPATIBILITY

Good luck in your search for love, and may the stars shine upon you in 2009!

Compatibility quick reference guide

Each of the twelve star signs has a greater or lesser affinity with one another. The quick reference guide on page 30 will show you who's hot and who's not so hot as far as your relationships are concerned.

SCORPIO + ARIES
Water + Fire = Steam

Here we have a combination of two very fiery and independent individuals and therefore head-on collisions are not out of the question for you.

Power is the name of the game when you combine these forces. Harnessing this power is important and will determine the outcome of your relationship. In some cases a battle of wills is likely because an Arian has just as much fire and purposefulness as you have.

Aries are unambiguous in action. Although they are quite impulsive and lacking in finesse and depth as far as you are concerned, this can be quite a compelling friendship once you both choose to give it a go. You will immediately be attracted to the passionate and sexual side of each other.

Scorpio will excite the hot-headed Aries, and they will boost your desire to explore new possibilities. You're both strong-willed individuals with daring personalities, so compromise is important if you are to make a go of it.

Both of you love a challenge, but your intuition will make you more restrained whereas Aries likes to be the fool that rushes in without thinking. Aries must never assume that Scorpio is a pushover. Your intricate and complex personality

SCORPIO

Quick reference guide: Horoscope compatibility between signs (percentage)

	Aries	Taurus	Gemini	Cancer	Leo	Virgo	Libra	Scorpio	Sagittarius	Capricorn	Aquarius	Pisces
Aries	60	65	65	65	90	45	70	80	90	50	55	65
Taurus	60	70	70	80	70	90	75	85	50	95	80	85
Gemini	70	70	75	60	80	75	90	60	75	50	90	50
Cancer	65	80	60	75	70	75	60	95	55	45	90	90
Leo	90	70	80	70	85	75	65	75	95	45	70	75
Virgo	45	90	75	75	75	70	80	85	70	95	50	70
Libra	70	75	90	60	65	80	80	85	80	85	95	50
Scorpio	80	85	60	95	75	85	85	90	85	65	60	95
Sagittarius	90	50	75	55	95	70	80	85	55	55	60	75
Capricorn	50	95	50	45	45	95	85	65	55	85	70	85
Aquarius	55	80	90	70	70	50	95	60	60	70	80	55
Pisces	65	85	50	90	75	70	50	95	75	85	55	80

requires a deep and penetrating mind. Not all Aries can handle that.

Aries are constantly on the go and are sometimes social butterflies. You, on the other hand, being a secretive and private person, want your home to be a sanctuary rather than a crash pad for a bunch of strangers. This will create conflict domestically.

Your passion is exciting together, and intimacy will be rewarding. Aries is sometimes impulsive and superficial in the bedroom but they still excite you. Sex is equally important to Scorpio and Aries and both exhibit similar drives to satisfy their primal urges.

You will often be at cross-purposes in life because you are both so fiercely determined and self-centred. One of you will need to rule the roost, so the question is who? On the other hand, this could give you a first-rate opportunity to make up intimately after your confrontational episodes.

There's never a dull moment with Aries born between 21 and 30 March. Here are combative types who will challenge you every step of the way. They will not take to your emotional control games. Give them the space they need, and your sexual relationship will more than make up for these other issues.

Those Aries born between 31 March and 10 April will be dominating types, especially in professional activities, which will seriously obstruct your desire to be in charge. This could be a disastrous combination if you don't like submitting yourself to someone else.

Aries born between 11 and 20 April are the best match under this star sign, because they have Jupiter and Sagittarius co-ruling them. You have strong emotional and karmic connections with them and can enjoy a fulfilling relationship together.

SCORPIO + TAURUS

Water + Earth = Mud

Both of you are attracted sexually but not necessarily emotionally or spiritually. Your attraction stems from the fact that you are both opposite signs and have considerable magnetic appeal for each other. Taurus being dynamic though not verbal reflects your own secretiveness. You feel passionate in their company. There's an undeniable attraction between you. They feel the same way about you, because of the sexy connection between Mars and Venus, your ruling planets.

Taurus hates ambiguity and can feel you are far too complex and emotionally difficult to deal with. You are a challenge for Taurus, but they are up to the challenge of Scorpio. Your inflexibility and their stubbornness is a recipe for conflict. You'll often drive each other crazy convincing the other of your own viewpoint. You need to respect each other's opinions.

You have a love of adventure whereas Taurus is concerned with the tried and tested. You are very mystical, whereas Taurus is practical. You could also find yourselves at odds financially. The relationship will bring up differences in the way you manage money. Power and control are the key words in your partnership. Although you'll nurture and love each other, such issues will be a major testing ground. Don't let them get in the way of developing a deeper love for one other.

Taurus may not trust you because they wear their hearts on their sleeves. You prefer to keep things buried deep within your heart. Taurus sees this as two-faced behaviour and will suffer for it. Your constant need to express yourself through sex will flatter Taurus but they are touchy-feely by nature and don't want only sex!

Communication between you is quite different. You like innuendoes and sometimes skirt the topic whereas Taurus calls a spade a spade. You find them a little boring and they find you complicated. Scorpios love the dark equally as much as the light. Taurus sees this as deviousness but you see it as an intrinsic part of human nature, growth and evolution of the spirit. The bull is extremely possessive, like you. This could cause no end of problems in your relationship, particularly if you are married.

Most Taureans do well with you; however, those born between 21 and 29 April are by far your best mates. A true love match is possible and marriage is quite likely with them.

You will be attracted to Taureans born between 30 April and 10 May, but this is more a platonic than sexual relationship. They are better suited to a social connection with you. You will not feel comfortable about taking this friendship to the next level.

Business between you and those born between 11 and 21 May will to well. However, before getting too involved, be sure you clearly understand your fine natal differences so you can satisfy their need for security. Once this part of the relationship is sorted out, the emotional and sexual aspects will look after themselves.

SCORPIO + GEMINI
Water + Air = Rain

This truly is one of the least-compatible combinations of the zodiac, so be prepared for some intense times. Gemini is light-hearted, frivolous and intellectual. They are flighty and occasionally irrational in your opinion. The way you communicate is different and you do not enjoy their frivolousness.

Gemini is clever and you are, too. You'll be constantly waging your wits against each other and testing your intellectual prowess, one on one. Geminis are chatterboxes. They love to talk and communicate their ideas. You on the other hand hold your cards close to your chest. You are intense about

SCORPIO

everything you do. Gemini prefers to spread themselves thinly, dabbling in a multitude of activities. You find their dispersed approach distracting.

Gemini is attracted to Scorpio but is not ultimately satisfied by you. They are forever young at heart due Mercury, the youthful planet. Some Scorpios, not all, are also able to maintain a vigorous and youthful approach to life. If that's the case, a Scorpio–Gemini match will be somewhat better.

Gemini will play with you, please you, yet will often infuriate you. If you retaliate and take yourself too seriously, you will be pained by this relationship. You must assume that it is the Gemini humour at work and not their desire to hurt or undermine you in any way. A sexual relationship between you can be playful and at the same time powerful. Here again you must go with the flow and get into the groove of the Gemini sense of humour if you are to enjoy this relationship fully.

Keep in mind that not all Geminis are as shallow as they first appear; they are just less intense than you. Your possessive and jealous streak won't sit too well with them. A good deal of adjustment is necessary if you are to strike a happy balance.

Geminis born between 22 May and 1 June will offer you loads of wit, charm and laughter. The other side of the coin is that these Geminis often live in their heads and find it difficult to express the passion you expect in a relationship. You will have to be patient and teach them about sex.

You are likely to splurge on Geminis born between 2 and 12 June. They bring out your generosity. It's probably better to avoid a long-term partnership with them unless you're thinking of going into business; a professional association would work well. You may meet through a work-related function or as a co-worker. This is a great combination for getting things done—a fine blend of Scorpio resolve and Gemini elegance.

Those born between 13 and 21 June will arouse many new interests and trigger the unconventional side of your personality. Because they are ruled partly by Uranus and Aquarius, they like to do things that have shock value. If you're prepared to go along for the ride, the journey will definitely be an interesting one.

SCORPIO + CANCER
Water + Water = Deluge

Scorpio and Cancer are both the same element of water so there is a natural affinity between you. However, both of you are possessive and jealous. You must control these emotions to bring the best out of your relationship. Essentially, Cancer would be regarded as one of the better astrological matches for your sign.

You are critical, and Cancer is sensitive to that criticism. Although you are both compatible, there is still be a lot of work to do on an emotional level. You are both extremely intuitive and sense each other's emotional swings. This is a distinct advantage in making the relationship a positive one. Your karma is also strong, which is why star signs of the same element are usually drawn together. You will be able to work together.

Cancer is happy with simple things but you tend to complicate their needs, which will make them unhappy if you don't allow them simply to be who they are. Try to flow more with Cancer's mood. The water signs take time to open up to each other and express the warmth of their personalities. Over time, with patience, you both will do this.

There's a strong sexual and magnetic appeal between you. You truly enjoy the energy that flows both ways. You enjoy sexual and emotional intrigue, but Cancer, with its love of home and family, needs anchoring and will eventually lead you

SCORPIO

to a more stable and domestic existence. You probably won't mind this and feel very comfortable about the domestic security they offer you.

Your lovemaking together is very fulfilling and mutually satisfying. You understand each other instinctively and know exactly what turns the other on.

Both of you are secretive and part of the lesson for you is to learn to share your deeper feelings with each other without fear of being hurt. You can do this more easily than Cancer as they are not as prone to vehemently attacking or hurting others as you are. Try the spare them the pain and grief by being more attuned to their sensitivity.

Cancers born between 22 June and 3 July don't possess the inner strength you desire in a person. They will, however, bring out the emotional side of your character. You do have a destiny together spiritually. You could work to help other people or simply to solve your own families' crises.

Cancers born between 4 and 13 July have a strong attraction for you and you for them. They will satisfy your complex needs. Both of you will be immediately attracted to each other, and your magnetic and sexual compatibility will be evident from the start.

Cancers born between 14 and 23 July have a lot going for them and are great fun. This group is strongly ruled by the Moon, and a relationship with them is a pretty good bet, especially if you consider yourself a party animal. You can kick up your heels and let down your guard with them.

SCORPIO + LEO
Water + Fire = Steam

The two of you are powerful star signs and therefore it's quite likely you will be attracted to each other due to the sexual

STAR SIGN COMPATIBILITY

intensity you both possess and exhibit. There is usually an immediate attraction and respect between you because of the innate strength of your star signs.

You have a certain amount of cynicism and sarcasm that will provoke Leo; but they can also be ferocious being the king of the jungle, so don't underestimate their capacity for retaliation. You will be surprised at the immense power they too possess.

You secretly desire love of the highest order and spend your life looking for it. You may not readily admit this, even to Leo, who attracts you very powerfully. Leo is flirtatious and this bothers you although you may not speak up to say so. By holding back secrets like this you run the risk of losing your Leo flame.

You are extremely competitive by nature and Leo is no different. My suggestion is that you keep your competitive instincts friendly and sporty. This way you will help rather than hinder each other. Otherwise this will also be a source of constant conflict for you.

Scorpios are instinctively protective of the ones they love and because Leo is quite capable of looking after him or herself, you could feel ineffectual with them. Even the lioness is self-sufficient and this will wound your ego. A Scorpio male is proud to have the Leo female by his side. She is the epitome of glamour, luxury and good taste. However, you mustn't use her like an accessory as you might view your car. Treat her with dignity and she will love you for keeps.

Leos have very big egos and need to take centre stage. Most Scorpios are private and secretive and this could produce some social discomfort for both of you. The lion radiates warmth, love and dramatic flair 24 hours a day, but you mustn't take this to be anything other than their desire to make sure that they are still appealing to the opposite sex. Your possessive and cynical attitude might read more into this: don't! A sexual relationship between you is excellent and you can expect many fun and fulfilling times intimately.

Leos born between 24 July and 4 August have large egos and can be quite opinionated. This will irritate you and make it hard for you to see eye to eye with them. One of you will have to be a little more submissive.

Scorpio is subtle about exerting power and control and likes to leave a little to the imagination, whereas Leo prefers to strut on centre stage. This contrast could be particularly strong with Leos born between 5 and 14 August, who need to sometimes exaggerate and make things far more theatrical than you like.

Leos born between 15 and 23 August are really well suited to a long-term partnership with you, as their temperament is in keeping with yours.

SCORPIO + VIRGO
Water + Earth = Mud

You'll feel comfortable with Virgo's principal urge to serve and fulfil your needs but you mustn't take this to mean that Virgo will sacrifice everything wholly and solely at your feet. That would be a grave mistake. Taking advantage of this virtue of Virgo won't do anything to enhance your relationship with them.

You are passionate and intensely loving towards Virgo, the virginal sign; however, they are not as demonstrative, at least not initially, and this could put you off before your romance even gets off the ground.

Virgo resists intense passion and sexual abandon probably because they are primarily about thoughts and rationalisation. Once they have a taste of your sexual world, however, their mind may indeed learn the art of switching off even it's only during these moments of intimacy.

Because you're deep and complex, the analytical antics of Virgo are at a loss to figure you out. You mustn't play on this but rather give them a hand in understanding you and this will endear them to you. You're mysterious enough to give them a few morsels of the unknown without compromising your persona.

Scorpio and Virgo can develop wonderful levels of communication and naturally empathise with each other. You are particularly well suited if you find common topics of interest or hobbies in which you will spend hours happily sharing your ideas. You will also work well together; you being the one who inspires Virgo into executing every detail of your plan. You will trust them implicitly.

Virgo is devout and loyal in family life and this is something you like as well. You feel secure and grounded with them. There is an unusual twist to the Scorpio and Virgo relationship in that Scorpio's problematic nature is an ideal quest for the analytical Virgo mind. It could take Virgo a lifetime to understand your enigmatic ways.

Be cautious of Virgos born between 24 August and 2 September: they have very different personalities to you. There will be arguments from time to time. There may also be a difference in your age or cultural background, which will make you question the relationship. Think hard about taking the friendship to a more serious level—*before* you dive in.

Virgos born between 3 and 12 September offer you gains and losses in equal measure, and many of your life lessons will be tied up in your financial relationship with them. Remember the saying 'Never mix business with pleasure'? If you can sort out this issue, these Virgos will offer you a solid and stable security that fits in with your personal view of life.

Virgos born between 13 and 23 September are ideally suited to long-term love and commitment. This is because Jupiter, which has a bearing on your romantic life and is a thoroughly lucky planet for you, also has a bearing on their destiny. You'll feel physically attracted to them, and will want a bright future with them.

SCORPIO + LIBRA
Water + Air = Rain

Although you are attracted to each other, it's highly unlikely that the refined Libra will be able to deal with your critical ways for a whole lifetime. You feel the need to reform Libra and this is your way of controlling them. But Librans can do this to themselves and will interpret your attempts to change them as egomania. Libra often points out your faults as well but they do this risking your vengeful responses. You must learn that if you want to change them you must be just as prepared to also be transformed by them.

Librans are indecisive in matters of love, whereas you know what you want. In fact, you demand what you want, and this is in contrast to the placid and amiable Libra. You will feel frustrated with the Libran yes–no responses. Libra also needs balance and a harmonious environment in which to prosper and grow emotionally. Your complicated mentality unnerves them and unsettles their way of life. You'll have to try harder to simplify your involvement with them.

Libran characters are full of charm and have strong social requirements. You must give this to them if your relationship is to prosper. Libra wants to explore open-ended social and romantic arrangements, so your possessive and demanding attitude will be too limiting for them. You need to reveal more of yourself, otherwise virtuous Libra will regard you as a contradiction morally. You are greatly mistaken if you think your facial expressions and eye movements will convey everything you're thinking to Libra. They need to hear your words of love verbally not just through your magical eyes, as magnetic and appealing as they are.

The female Libra is somewhat adaptable to the Scorpio male from a sexual point of view so this combination of male and female is a good one. The Libran male may not, however, be sexual enough for the Scorpio female, although they do have oodles of sensuality and charm. Unfortunately this may not compensate the Scorpion woman's innate needs sufficiently. Libra will sanctify the love act and lift you out of your base-instinctive, animal level to something pure and spiritual if you let them.

You need to be extremely cautious when involving yourself in a relationship with Librans born between 24 September and 3 October: your financial involvement with them could get messy because you have totally different approaches to the way money should be managed. Until you have a clear idea of each other's financial philosophy, don't get into loans or other borrowings together.

Librans born between 4 and 13 October are sometimes regarded as air heads. They're indecisive about things that you think should be more easily resolved. You are a quick decision maker and sometimes act against your own interests, while these Librans need to explore every possible alternative.

Librans born between 14 and 23 October will be great companions for you and will always support you with wise advice. This will be a good match and the communication level will be satisfying as well.

SCORPIO + SCORPIO
Water + Water = Deluge

The reason that a match between Scorpio and Scorpio can be either heaven or hell is because Scorpio traditionally has been known to produce both sinners and saints. On most levels you are extremely compatible; however, Scorpios range in three

SCORPIO

bands from the most base and crass to the most resulted and spiritually evolved among us.

Sexual passion is the basis of your relationship because your star sign rules such things as sexuality, intimacy, death, and transformation. It is through these human experiences that you will understand yourself more fully and also understand your partner. Your sexual appetite will quite likely be fulfilled within the relationship because only another Scorpio understands these deeper motivations.

Unfortunately people equate Scorpio's passion solely with the sexual aspect of life and this is only a very limited view of your star sign. As you know, passion is something you exhibit in everything you do, not just in lovemaking. You want a spiritual interaction in your relationships and that is why, when both of you are performing at your best, this relationship will be something quite unique, quite special.

On the flip side, both of you are suspicious by nature and very possessive and domineering of each other. You find it hard to give the other the unconditional freedom that should mark a relationship based on true love and understanding. You should never see each other as possessions.

Scorpio is the most secretive of the signs so one of your biggest lessons will be to share your feelings with more transparency. Hiding your emotions will only create more problems and could even bring forth the vindictive and vehement streak of Scorpio. Never hold grudges and practise the art of forgiveness. You should always kiss and make up before bed.

The Scorpio–Scorpio match usually results in a long-lasting relationship even though you both have complex personalities. Rather than being jealous of each other's activities, support one another and combine your power to develop an amazing relationship, not just a good one.

Scorpios born between 24 October and 2 November are instantly attracted to you. Their sexual appeal will be heightened as a result. Once you become involved with them, you could find yourselves joined at the hip because there is such a close resemblance in personality.

Your best combination is with Scorpios born between 3 November and 12 November. They are also ruled by Neptune and Pisces. These Scorpios provide you with everything you need to feel as if you're in the perfect relationship. They're idealistic, and believe that the most important thing in life is unconditional love.

You may have a gentler and more emotional relationship with Scorpios born between 13 and 22 November. This is because the Moon and Cancer filter through their personalities and bring out the very emotional side of your nature. They are soft, caring, and very family oriented. If it's family life you're after, these Scorpios will be ideal for you.

SCORPIO + SAGITTARIUS
Water + Fire = Steam

Both of you are very physically active and will enjoy outdoor life as part of your relationship. Your vitality stimulates each other and gives you a sense of wellbeing when you're in each other's company. Scorpio and Sagittarius can be great friends; their ruling planets are friendly. This is also a terrific love combination, and should be full of optimism and warmth. Both of you have a positive view of life and will want to accomplish a lot.

However, Sagittarius is idealistic in love and you are too intense and possessive. These are some differences that will need to be nutted out. Both of you are friendly and social by nature so it will to your benefit to work through them. You are secretive and don't always reveal what's on your mind. This is not exactly the best way to develop trust with someone who

SCORPIO

is so brutally honest. The downside is that your relationship can be explosive and an excessive one. Unless Sagittarius sticks to some basic emotional and mental ground rules, the partnership will burn out.

Fire and water don't necessarily make the best match due to an elemental mismatch. Scorpio's water dampens the enthusiastic fire of Sagittarius, and that would be a shame as Sagittarius needs a free rein to let their spirits soar. Sagittarius is also quite restless by nature whereas you seek permanence and need to control most elements of the relationship to feel comfortable. Sagittarius may not be amenable to this arrangement and compromise is necessary for you to both feel happy together in a relationship.

Sexually the two of you will get on very well and you enjoy the warmth of the Sagittarian personality. They love your intense love making! Whatever differences you have can be resolved. Scorpio is more sensitive than Sagittarius knows. Sagittarius has a frank and open style of discussing things so that simply pointing out a fault could deeply hurt you. If you're too secretive and don't let them know what's working for you and what's not, how are they supposed to know?

Communication is of paramount importance in this relationship. Because Sagittarius likes to share, your sex life can be exciting, but it could be one-sided until you become trusting and open enough with them. When you come out from behind your steely wall of self-preservation, Sagittarius will find your loving responses irresistible.

Any professional arrangements you have with Sagittarians born between 23 November and 1 December will lead to success, and will be positive for your financial arrangement as a couple.

Sagittarians born between 2 and 11 December will feel very connected to you: Mars is the planetary ruler for both of you, and gives you a very close physical relationship. Your sexual energies are very well matched.

STAR SIGN COMPATIBILITY

If you become attached to Sagittarians born between 12 and 22 December, there will be ego clashes, because they are wilful and egocentric individuals. Your competitive urges will be unpleasant. You'll need all your diplomacy skills to survive a relationship with them.

SCORPIO + CAPRICORN
Water + Earth = Mud

Although there are compatible and incompatible aspects to a Scorpio–Capricorn relationship, there are still some redeeming features to the partnership. Both of you have an initial luke-warm reaction to each other, with Capricorn being less demonstrative and passionate than you. You like to think of yourself as sexually exciting (but Scorpio can also be repressive at times).

You see the goat as undemonstrative and conservative in romance. Capricorn doesn't like to show emotion too quickly. They are not only economical with money and material commodities but with their affections as well. If both of you are holding back psychologically this will be a rather cold affair.

Both of you tend to brood and hold grudges. Your ruling planets are unfriendly to each other so this may cause a rift. One of you will have to step up to the plate and be the hero in this relationship. This is the only way the Scorpio–Capricorn match will grow.

Scorpio, you often exhibit a different face to your true character and this will unsettle Capricorn who has a very down-to-earth view of things. You mustn't play mind games with them because they won't give too much emphasis to your social or sexual secrets. They are primarily concerned with the concrete world of facts and figures. When they refuse to respond to your mystical manipulations you'll find yourself running out of ammunition against them.

SCORPIO

Some male Scorpios prefer not to demonstrate how they truly feel in a relationship. This is a mistake because they have so much passion and emotion to share but often don't and are therefore misunderstood. Capricorns are extremely loyal and trustworthy and because of this you will feel comfortable and less suspicious with them. Capricorns are also possessive to some extent, like yourself, and this two-way traffic of unhealthy emotion might also be a problem you will both have to confront.

Both of you are independent people and must give each other room for personal growth. Capricorns are shy and unassuming in the bedroom and may not fulfil your gargantuan sexual appetite. You both must avoid monotony, otherwise the relationship will grind to a halt.

Capricorns born between 23 December and 1 January will stifle you. You won't feel confident that you really understand them—that's because they have a double-dose of Saturn ruling them. This makes them conservative and unlikely to share their feelings with you that easily.

Capricorns born between 2 and 10 January are a good match for you because they have sexy and loving Venus influencing them. In fact, their affectionate nature will make you wonder whether these people are really Capricorns at all.

Friendship and a great social life are on the cards with Capricorns born between 11 and 20 January, but deep down you feel that you don't really know them. They have two very different sides to their character; one is outgoing, the other secretive. Not unlike you, is it?

SCORPIO + AQUARIUS
Water + Air = Rain

Scorpio and Aquarius are both flirtatious by nature but in very different ways. Scorpio uses charm to test others but Aquarius

STAR SIGN COMPATIBILITY

is more prone to take flirtation to the next level. This relationship could be painful if you're intense possessiveness is not curbed. You could find it hard to deal with the free-wheeling-and-dealing Aquarian, the new-age character of the zodiac.

Aquarius is aloof and detached in matters of love, whereas sexually you are emotionally deep and attached. Aquarius will not cope with your suspicious and possessive nature if you try to control them and superimpose your version of love and romance on their character.

Both of you are fixed signs and are therefore opinionated and often at cross-purposes in many areas of life. You're both determined individuals and stick to whatever you take on until you have completed the task. Also, neither of you aren't afraid of challenges. This is usually essential in terms of a relationship's durability; but in this relationship, it may be the opposite: the more you dig your heels in, the less chance it will work.

Scorpio is mystical; Aquarius is as well but not in the same, obsessive way. Deeper spiritual connectivity in your relationship will be like fine wine that is maturing with age, so don't expect fireworks at the outset. The rewards in this relationship will take time to be realised, so be patient.

Aquarius is an eccentric sign and this attracts you. Later you might find it hard to deal with the quirky attitude and behaviour of Aquarius. Aquarius is experimental, however, and this will satisfy you sexually. You both are confident in the bedroom and whatever incompatibility arises between you can also be overcome through your adventurous nature.

Both of you are supremely intuitive, with Scorpio being more the secretive sign. Share some of your insights with Aquarius and this will help cement the bonds of love between you. You should never be spiteful in your arguments with Aquarius. They prefer logical and deductive discussion rather than hurtful emotional digs.

SCORPIO

Scorpio, you will secretly disapprove of the Aquarian individuality but you should speak up about this problem. Aquarius needs to know that you support their unique personality and that you do so unconditionally.

Aquarians born between 21 January and 31 January are quite restless individuals. They are likely to change their opinions as often as the wind changes. Secondly, they can be rather explosive types. This means it will be hard for the two of you to see eye to eye.

Aquarians born between 1 February and 8 February have a rather unusual communication style. Because you are not always open in expressing your feelings, this could be a complicated relationship at times.

An excellent choice for romance and marriage is with Aquarians born between 9 February and 19 February. They are influenced by Venus and Libra. This makes them not only intellectual, but also sensual and emotional. You will enjoy your intimate expressions together.

SCORPIO + PISCES
Water + Water = Deluge

Destiny will bring you to each other and your relationship is no accident. You probably already know that. This is a mysterious relationship and one with very strong karmic bonds. You'll both learn many lessons together.

Strangely, however, even though both of you fall under the same water element, the Scorpion will never survive in the realm of water. It is, after all, a land creature. You'll have to learn how to swim with the fish!

You're inspirational to Pisces and their unconditional love will cause you to rise to their level and fully open up your heart. You'll fulfil every need of Pisces—particularly their sexual desires. In return they will do the same.

STAR SIGN COMPATIBILITY

Pisceans are incorrigible flirts and your unforgiving nature may hurt them if you retaliate, especially if they believe their behaviour is harmless and not impacting upon the relationship. Pisces is not secretive like you but does tend to live in a world of its own.

Their supreme spiritual vibrations cause Pisces to be self-absorbed much of the time. This may make them appear secretive to you, very much mirroring your own behaviour. This is probably quite an annoying feeling, that they reflect the very thing you detest, the secretive part of your own character!

Pisces are not quite as financially savvy as you. Monetary issues and squabbles over money are likely. Pisces is generous to a fault and you find this difficult to square up. You like money and the power that it affords you whereas Pisces sees this as a means of carrying out altruistic and humanitarian assistance to others.

Because Scorpio is an energetic and ambitious sign, Pisces might seem a little insipid and lacking in general drive and energy to you. You may have to constantly motivate Pisces far too much for your liking or theirs. Your drives are very different, with Pisces aspiring to nebulous and otherworldly objectives. You like being grounded.

Scorpio and Pisces often marry and have a good chance of making the relationship special. For example, take Elizabeth Taylor and Richard Burton. This famous Pisces–Scorpio match was always destined for love, passion and also separation and pain. Yearning for each other's company will be part and parcel of your life together. Under any circumstances, though, it's best for Scorpio Pisces to stay with each other.

You'll have strong bonds of love and sensual satisfaction with Pisces born between 20 and 28 or 29 February. They are double-Pisces, and their compassionate and idealistic personalities will soothe your soul.

SCORPIO

Your karmic connection with Pisces born between 1 and 10 March is very powerful. Cancer and the Moon have a great deal of influence on them. You could learn a lot about your emotional self with these Pisces.

Extremes in passion occur when Scorpio connects with Pisces born between 11 and 20 March, because they also have strong Scorpio tendencies. This is a very powerful, but also at times tumultuous, combination.

SCORPIO

2009: The Year Ahead

SCORPIO

When all else is lost, the future still remains.

—Christian Nestell Bovee

Romance and friendship

This last couple of years has been an incredibly uplifting time on all fronts for Scorpio. Professionally and romantically you feel as if you are now ready to move on to the next stage of your life for bigger and better things.

As the year commences the majority of planets are located in the practical sign of Capricorn and the progressive sign of Aquarius. This refers to practicality versus freethinking and independence. You want freedom but will not allow anything to stand in the road of your financial security, either.

With Venus, the planet of love and long-term and committed relationships being in Aquarius, you are keen to add spice to your love life and are not interested in anything that will hinder you from experiencing the passion that is your true nature during the coming twelve months.

This is highlighted after the 3rd of January when Venus produces wonderful romantic prospects for you by influencing your zone of love affairs and your personal esteem. And, what's more, there is a dose of intense Pluto energy giving you the impetus to transform current relationships or go all out to try something uniquely different. The first part of the year certainly makes you attractive to the opposite sex and there's every chance that single Scorpios will be off to a good start in 2009 with planetary factors indicating good luck.

Jupiter joins Neptune in your zone of family and domestic affairs around the same time, on the 6th of January, and this introduces a twelve-month period where much of your focus will be turned on your family members with a view to improving your closest relationships. This is an excellent time to bury the hatchet and resolve your differences so that your conscience is clear and home life is more relaxed. You've probably been a busy bee for some time and this has impacted upon your personal affairs. Now you are able to give your loved ones the attention they deserve.

There are some hurdles to overcome in February when Venus and Pluto enter a challenging phase, but fortunately this doesn't last long, so you must be careful not to jump to conclusions and assume that things are worse than they are, romantically speaking. By the 18th, when Venus and Jupiter create favourable energies for you, things will settle down both in your love life and your social affairs. It's likely some disputes or at least differences of opinion could get you and your friends hot under the collar during this period so try to keep a balanced mind and not make too much of what others are saying. You are likely to take statements a little too personally for your own good. Let their words pass over like water on a duck's back.

In March your eyes will be on greener pastures and you mustn't let this contentment cause you to step outside a long-standing relationship just for the sake of a little excitement. You could regret it afterwards.

Between the 7th and 15th, when Venus goes retrograde, all sorts of strange things may occur in your relationships. Mixed signals could make you feel as if others don't care and that you're putting in much more than you are receiving. Loved ones may seem distant or disconnected from you. Again, you mustn't take these natural fluctuations in relationships too personally. Just go with the flow until Venus resumes its normal course around the middle of April.

You want excitement in April but the adverse combination of Mars and Saturn puts the brakes on and so frustration could set in and your dreams may need to be put on hold for just a little while. More serious responsibilities and a sense of unconditional service will colour your relationships at this

SCORPIO

time. You mustn't expect to receive as much as you will need to give. If you follow the natural trend of the planets you can gain some deeper spiritual fulfilment from your friendships and closest relationships.

At this time someone close to you may suffer some health crisis and you will also be called upon to render assistance to your best capacity. Your compassion will be strong during this phase and you'll learn some valuable lessons about the true meaning of love.

Your spirits are lifted when the Sun enters your most important zone of relationships on the 20th of April. Enjoy the radiant vibrations because your relationships are elevated to a new high. New partnerships and friendships are forecast for you at this time and, if you happen to be in an existing relationship, the solar energy is will draw you closer together and give you a renewed sense of love and intimacy.

Your sexual affairs are spotlighted throughout the period of May and June and this is due to the influence of Mercury and the Sun entering a transformative and sexual zone of your horoscope. This is a time of playfulness, experimentation and progressive analysis of how your emotions and sexuality are working with your partner's. With Mercury's retrogression or reverse movement, some unusual happenings are likely in this respect.

Any new relationship that is started now may get off to a shaky start and, if it is particularly based upon physical and sexual connections, it is likely to disappoint you. It's best to wait till this planet has moved into a more direct motion before giving your approval and committing yourself to someone, especially if initially they are strangers.

This is not all about sex, however, and the middle portion of the year can reveal many new facets about your inner desires and those of your partner as well. During June and July, Venus

2009: THE YEAR AHEAD

and Mars commence a very powerful cycle where their combined energy affects your passion very strongly.

For Scorpio this is an incredibly intense phase and, if your passions are not fully reciprocated by the one you love, some important or should I say drastic changes take place for the sake of fulfilling these very primal instincts. Scorpio is after all the most sexual sign of the zodiac.

This combination of energies reaches a peak in the last week of June so I only hope you have someone with which to share these most intimate moments. The power of Venus and Mars continues to influence you and your spouse or partner powerfully throughout August as well, so this three-month period should be a memorable one for you.

Saturn's influence is undeniable this year and its action will be primarily felt on your most important friendships. This is highlighted throughout the period of September and October, just before it makes an important transition out of your zone of friendships. Any outmoded relationships will need to be discarded, and you will know which ones I am talking about.

Have you been with people that are hanging on, using your goodwill and not reciprocating in the way they should? You will realise at this point that any friendship or love affair has to be built on mutual give and take. Unfortunately some of your relationships to date have not been founded on this important principle. As Saturn moves out of this sector, a new two-and-a-half-year cycle gets underway and it is likely you will seek a whole new circle of friends and acquaintances that are better in keeping with whom you have become as a person. In other words, this is primarily an important spiritual development for most Scorpios at this time.

The latter part of 2009 will be largely coloured by this very significant Saturnine influence. Some of you who are not accustomed to letting relationships slip by that easily will be a

SCORPIO

little down in the dumps for a while, but not for long. With Uranus spending considerable time in your area of love affairs, you will continue to seek novel and unusual people who can satisfy your yearning for something just that little bit different.

In November, when Venus transits your Sun sign, your grace and charm will be attractive enough to bring to you many new acquaintances who will renew your self-confidence. Some Scorpios will even be fortunate enough to come in touch with their soulmates. One of your ruling planets, Mars, also reaches the zenith of the heavens, giving you the supreme self-confidence and the ability to take from life what you believe is yours.

As the year draws to a conclusion, the idealistic Jupiter and Neptune bless you with a new vision of who you are and what you truly deserve in life. You'll come to understand that life is to be lived and that each moment is precious. There's no time to waste in relationships and with people who are not as passionate and loving as you. Fortunately a new phase commences in which just the right type of characters will be drawn to you on your life path, and I can safely predict that they will positively affect your destiny for a long time to come. Good luck in 2009!

Work and money

There comes a time in everyone's life when they must choose between money and doing what they truly love. During this most important year of 2009, the true yearning to follow your heart's dream will become stronger and stronger.

Your career planet, the Sun, is surrounded by friendly Mars and Jupiter, which is an excellent omen indicating this will be a fortunate year, financially and professionally, for you. In particular, your communication style will be more open and cordial. Scorpio is known to be a little brash and less than diplomatic in approach.

2009: THE YEAR AHEAD

This will definitely change in the coming year and it will make life much easier for you. People are more receptive to your sales and business pitches. You are even likely to negotiate better deals for day-to-day items due to your affable and charming ways.

Make a concerted effort to settle any contracts in January. You have the power of persuasion and can do so easily. Advertise your services and use the power of Mercury and Jupiter to achieve your goals or at least make important headway in the first few weeks of the year. This will hold you in good stead.

Although the Sun is in the lower part of your horoscope throughout February and March, it is an opportunity for you to quietly and effectively plan and organise the coming year. Many Scorpios will be working behind the scenes and mustering all the strength they need in the second and third quarters of the year.

Responsibilities could weigh heavily upon your shoulders in the latter part of March and, unless you are able to manage your workload, your health may give you a few problems throughout April. Try to balance your working hours with your personal commitments so that you don't overdo it. You may also have problems with co-workers throughout April and May. Continue to use your diplomatic skills to sidestep problems that could become long-term if you are too reactive.

In the second half of May new business partnerships will be attractive and you can achieve something of lasting value in the way of new commercial contacts. Those of you who work as consultants, agents or salespeople can look forward to some brilliant results because the response of your clients will be exactly what you're after.

By carefully negotiating your shared finances and assets throughout June and July, you will achieve a great deal more financial stability. Setting clear guidelines will be essential, however. You may need to engage the services of experienced

SCORPIO

professionals to help you break old habits. The problem as I see it is that you or others may not be amenable to utilising new accounting principles and techniques for streamlining these aspects of your life.

Saturn has a restricting influence on the profitability of your ventures and requires you to be frugal or less extravagant with whatever money you have. This may have impacted upon you in a way that has made you feel less than grateful for what you have. During this cycle of Mercury in your eighth zone of shared resources, some important and positive news will turn things around for you.

As I said earlier in your romance forecast, when Saturn moves to the all-important expense sector of your horoscope in November, many of these problems will disappear but you must be diligent, especially throughout August, September and October to utilise fully the benefits that come to you after this. If you squander your money, of what use is that?

Venus brings with it immense luck in your professional sphere throughout September. Irrespective of your financial concerns I can safely say that the impact upon your working life will be most favourable. Jupiter also influences your working life at this time, so it's likely you will be promoted or may even have an opportunity to pursue a career of your choice.

Your professional objectives can be achieved throughout October when Venus and Mercury combine with Saturn in the zone of friendships and life fulfilment. You can expect an increase in salary, or some special support or attention from your bosses or superiors during this phase. But the all-important transit is in November when your co-ruling planet Mars dashes into your career zone, with stellar results.

Your leadership ambitions (if you have them) will be realised at this late stage of the year. Even if you don't happen to be a career-minded person, you can make a formidable impression wherever you are. At home you will finally be able to effect the changes that give you back some of your power and self-respect, especially if others have been treating you like a doormat.

Mars continues its journey in your career zone so the last month of the year crowns you with success. Moreover, with Venus, the Sun and Mercury tenanting your zone of income, money is spotlighted and constructively so. It doesn't appear that Christmas will faze you; quite the contrary, you can look forward to plenty of spare cash to splurge on your loved ones during the festive season.

Karma, luck and meditation

Your luck is associated with your powers of persuasion; to convince others to give you pretty much whatever you want this year. No one will argue with you too much and that's clear from the placement of your friendly planets in the third zone of communication in the early part of 2009. A fortuitous journey is also likely early in the year, and if the offer is made even casually, don't refuse. Opportunities arise when you least expect it.

Your luck changes around March when most of the planets occupy your domestic sphere. Building a better house, purchasing land or considering a career in real estate might provide you with some lucky opportunities for better income and a far more satisfying lifestyle.

Speculation brings some sudden and possibly even sizeable gains after April. Mars and Uranus are often sudden in action and the tip you receive from a friend is likely to pay off handsomely. Don't make a habit of gambling but this is one time you might like to wager at least a small bet on the horses or at the local casino.

Romance is favourable throughout June and July so be available when Mr or Ms Right comes walking through the door. However, you mustn't let your passion blind you to the deeper and more significant aspects of the relationship.

SCORPIO

Venus has strong links to your professional opportunities during September. For those of you who have been waiting patiently for a promotion, the period from September to December should be very constructive, indeed. On the other hand, a change is as good as a holiday and this is the time to venture out into new work if you feel it's time to move on. You'll be lucky in any sort of interview at this time.

… SCORPIO

2009: Month by Month Predictions

JANUARY

My interest is in the future because I am going to spend the rest of my life there.

—Charles F. Kettering

Highlights of the month

In the early part of the month you get off to a great start and between the 1st and the 5th your social life will skyrocket. January is certainly an exciting period for you when new love affairs are likely to surface. There is an air of intensity to your emotional life due to the effects of Pluto on you. You will not be interested in anything casual just now so be careful because your power and passion may be just a little too much for newcomers to handle.

Your domestic life is spotlighted between the 6th and the 12th; however, the influence of Jupiter entering your domestic zone will be felt for at least the next twelve months. Dealings with relatives, siblings and most importantly your mother and father will take centre stage. You will need to put aside some time to deal with these issues and resolve any outstanding matters.

For some Scorpios, this can be a therapeutic period psychologically and emotionally because Jupiter has the ability to heal old wounds and bring friendship back into the picture. If you've been at odds with someone you love I'm pleased to say that this period will relieve you of a lot of frustration and turbulence that might previously have been a feature of your life.

During the period of the 16th to the 25th I see you regaining your sense of confidence and connectedness to family life. If you're a man who happens to be working long hours, feeling that you haven't been able to dedicate the time necessary to your loved ones, a change in your routine will give you the chance to prove your love once again by being there for them.

You can expect several romantic opportunities to arise between the new Moon of the 26th and the 30th. Meetings with older people and those of the opposite sex will be surprisingly satisfying. Far from these older individuals being boring, you will experience a refreshing new perspective on friendship and a possible romance. You can learn a lot from those you meet in the second and third week of January.

If you are a single Scorpio, this period is exciting because you may stumble upon someone special. I could even go so far as to say this might be your soulmate. You will find so much in common with those you meet now that it will be almost too good to be true.

You have the ability to persuade others to think along your lines and in your business life this is an excellent month finally to put to bed any outstanding contracts or deals that have been hanging around. This is a month to get the monkey off your back and shine professionally and financially.

Romance and friendship

You're earthy on the 5th and want to stay in and stay grounded rather than going out and mixing with the world. You'll probably feel slower than normal as well, so you should go with the flow and not force yourself into any social situation

SCORPIO

that doesn't feel quite right. Entertaining at home is preferable. It should be quiet until the 9th.

Between the 12th and 14th you must pick your moments if you wish to be more economical as others will brand you as a scrooge. Hold back on unnecessary spending in private and then if necessary splurge a little on your friends. It's quite likely that under this current cycle you will be feeling a little more conscious of security and your future financial position.

It's nice to know you have friends but there is a dilemma when choices have to be made between one or the other and this can be a difficult call. One solution is to decline an offer from both so as not to offend either of them. Use your discrimination wisely on the 16th.

There may also be news of a birth between the 18th and the 21st—not necessarily within your own family circle but from someone you know—and this will make you happy. Expect a celebration or two at this time.

You probably want to feel more creative now but when you actually sit down and figure out what it is you would like to do, you find yourself scratching your head. You need to set aside time to investigate what is out there and what fits with who you are. This will be an interesting cycle, especially between the new Moon of the 26th and the 30th. Do a little research before engaging with others.

Work and money

Finances continue to take centre stage between the 3rd and the 8th and your attention to these matters will pay off handsomely. A careful reshuffle of the way you're banking and saving money, paying your mortgage or other term payments is the key to growing your nest egg effectively just at this time. Take a second look at how you manage your finances.

2009: JANUARY

You're worried about your health and the costs that may be involved from the 10th to the 15th, possibly because your health fund doesn't cover some of these aspects; for example, dental, osteopathic or other alternative practices. You will need to revisit this issue so that you don't get caught out on paying larger and larger gaps in your medical bills. Incidentally, these issues could also extend to your home insurance as well, especially by the 20th.

You may find yourself overwhelmed by paper work around the 24th and unfortunately sometimes the only free time you have is on a weekend. If you've overlooked your taxation records or have found yourself sweeping this issue under the rug for way too long, you may have to bite the bullet and immerse yourself in some unpalatable work at this time.

Destiny dates

Positive: 1, 2, 3, 4, 5, 6, 7, 8, 9, 17, 18, 19, 20, 21, 22, 23, 25, 26, 27, 28, 29, 30

Negative: 13, 14, 15

Mixed: 10, 11, 12, 16, 24

FEBRUARY

Highlights of the month

Around the full Moon of the 9th there will be some issues to deal with in your relationships. Venus and Pluto create some difficult romantic problems for you but only if you jump to conclusions. Things are never as bad as they seem and even if they are a little worse than you expect there are ways and means of approaching a situation and calmly working through them to a solution.

Between the 14th and the 18th you will realise that there are some people you have been associated with who are not particularly beneficial to either your emotional or professional wellbeing. You will have to make a tough call and remove these people from your life. That becomes difficult if they happen to be working with you and you're not in a position to leave your job. In this case your diplomatic skills will be called into action so that you can balance this rather difficult situation.

On the 20th you could be extremely reactive so try not to take a person's advice or opinion too personally as it may not be intended to wound your ego. Listen to what they have to say and take it with a grain of salt. On the 22nd you could find yourself dealing with someone who thinks they know much more about you than you do! They are probably confused in their own lives and need someone to point their finger at. You have to exercise compassion and see them for who they are.

By the new Moon of the 25th your relationships are strongly focused. The planets Venus and Jupiter take your relationships and friendships to another level. This is possible only after confronting one or two of your closest friends on issues that may have been bothering you. I can't rule out arguments where differences of opinion could get out of hand. You will need to control yourself even if they lose their cool.

With the Sun moving in the domestic sphere of your horoscope this month it's not a bad idea to take stock of yourself and in a particular your professional activities to make some hushed changes. There's no need to advertise the fact, so quietly work away at adjusting those things you feel may be obstructing your success.

Sometime around the 28th a journey you've hankered for is likely to be possible and you will fulfil a desire you may have cherished for some time. It could be a place that has captivated your attention and imagination and you will have some link karmically with that place. I wouldn't be surprised that, for some of you, your life is destined to be connected to this location.

Romance and friendship

You definitely need to pull out the old box of postcards, photographs and other knick knacks and reminisce a little around the 6th and 7th. Over coffee or lunch you will want to do this with a friend or close family member and recollect the old times—good and bad—from yesteryear. You'll be feeling very nostalgic during this cycle and will want to make contact with an old friend or two.

On the 13th your words will cut if you are not sensitive enough to the company you find yourself in. Be mindful of the fact that not everyone can digest your straightforward

SCORPIO

opinions, regardless of how honest *you* feel you are. It's a matter of sugar-coating your statements and opinions before making your point. Don't be so hard on others.

Deep thinking will help you arrive at some important conclusions about your life during the period of the 19th to the 22nd. Your imagination will soar so you mustn't allow yourself to be limited by what others feel you can or can't do. It's up to you to believe in yourself and push forward to your goal, even if it seems a little unrealistic at the moment.

Around the 21st a fortuitous journey is likely to captivate your attention. If an invitation is offered even casually, don't refuse. Romantic opportunities arise when you least expect it.

It's a romantic stalemate for some Scorpios between the 24th and the 26th, and this is all a matter of ego and pride. Who cares who's wrong and who's right? Make some love not war even if you feel as though you've been wronged. The important point is that life is too short to miss even a precious moment of it. It's time to kiss and make up.

Work and money

A combination of lucky breaks in your financial affairs as well as repayments of owed money to you will result in a far better financial situation during the period of the 10th to the 17th. What will you do with the surplus cash? I suspect and also recommend you pamper yourself a little and go out and have a good time to send out a positive signal to the universe that you deserve the best.

Transport and other travel issues are high on your agenda from the 19th till the 22nd and the good news is that someone who performs a service (car service?) for you will be overly generous, offering you a discount rate on the job or the repairs. Also, make sure your home and contents insurance policies are up to date and the figure reflects the value of things you have acquired over the past year.

You are very intense about completing your chores and might find yourself feeling run down around the 27th. Remember, life is not a race and actually there are no pressures from anyone else other than yourself just now. Pace yourself and enjoy the work you do.

Destiny dates

Positive: 6, 7, 10, 11, 12, 19, 20, 21, 22, 28

Negative: 9, 18, 24, 26, 27

Mixed: 13, 14, 15, 16, 17, 25

MARCH

Highlights of the month

You're lucky during March and this is primarily associated with your internal state rather than any external situation. That being said, you are likely to want to externalise your inner contentment and in some cases this will mean putting your roots down by changing residence, purchasing a house or at least renovating your current dwelling so that this will reflect more accurately who you are.

This is a month when your lifestyle comes into clear focus and you will be asking yourself the question: 'Is this really how I want to live or is there a better way?' Remember not to place too much emphasis on the money aspect. The secret of success is to live a life of love and passion and from that money naturally flows.

Banking issues will be on the agenda between the 3rd and the 5th and, if you are looking to secure a loan for a new car, a house or other personal effect, this is the time to make an appointment and front the bank manager with the question. You are likely to be extravagant and this is highlighted by the full Moon in your 12th zone of expenses and charitable deeds. Remember that charity begins at home and that you must secure your own future before you can help anyone else.

Between the 7th and 15th Venus throws you a curved ball as far as your relationships are concerned. Your friends and partners will not be clear on what they want and this will cause you some emotional turmoil. The reason for this is that they are probably working through some of their own issues and you are reading too much into the picture. Of course they may be a little distant and aloof but give them space until Venus moves into its normal course next month.

Your financial opportunities to increase income and provide you with this lifestyle we are talking about take place between the 16th and the 23rd. There's nothing magical about this additional source of income, however, because it's most likely to be a case of you working harder with extra hours being put in at the office.

Around the 25th you'll be wondering whether the current situation you are in romantically is fulfilling enough. As a Scorpio you do have an insatiable appetite for affection, romance and sensual and sexual fulfilment. If your partner isn't reciprocating, you're likely to consider the alternatives. On the other hand you will need time to compare and appraise whether or not you are compatible enough with a newcomer in your life. As long as your actions are transparent this will actually be a good thing for you.

From the new Moon of the 26th your work responsibilities could create some health problems for you and if not checked now could reach a peak next month. Pull back your working hours and if you have too many personal commitments postpone a few of them. Your health is priceless and everything else can wait.

Romance and friendship

On the 3rd you may be confused as to why someone has given you what you thought was a green light emotionally only to pull the plug at the 11th hour. You mustn't keep sending

SCORPIO

e-mails or messages as this will make you seem far too needy. Back off a little bit and play a little harder to get. If that doesn't work, it's time to move on to greener pastures.

Someone's compliments will make you feel needed and much more confident about your social skills between the 9th and the 11th. It's quite likely you feel less capable than you are. It's time to create positive thoughts about your own self and project just how great you are. Your ideas of inadequacy is all self-created.

If you are particularly concerned about your health or that of another on the 12th, there's no point worrying yourself until you actually are ill. Do the right thing and get a check up to make sure that there is no medical problem. You're probably making a mountain out of a mole hill, anyway.

An impromptu departure from your home on the 18th may be a little irritating but will later turn out to be a blessing in disguise. Be prepared to change your plans at a moment's notice and with someone you would least expect. An unconventional relationship is also on the cards around the 23rd and should be exciting, to say the least.

Be careful of conflicts with friends on the 27th. The energy in the air is hot and thick and all parties concerned are likely to be over-reactive. You may find yourself confronted by a situation or a person whom you'd rather avoid but may not be able to. Under the circumstances you will simply have to grin and bear it.

Work and money

If you're feeling worried about completing your assignments and doing a good job, you need to allocate more time to your studies this month, particularly between the 7th and the 9th. You have swept some of your deadlines under the rug just when you knew that you had to lift your performance (not slacken off). There's still time to complete the task.

2009: MARCH

You are uncertain about a course of action but needn't be. It's all a matter of trusting your own intuition, not what others are telling you. By the 14th, you'll muster up the strength to tell someone to butt out of your affairs if you feel they've been interfering. This added strength will also be useful in juggling your studies, work and family life.

You have a lot of business to conduct but not quite enough time to get it all done. Communication is hectic, particularly between the 18th and the 25th. Make sure your diary has enough room to accommodate all these new appointments.

Your financial affairs are also on the upswing with Mercury, the Sun and Jupiter helping you blast your way into some new business circles around the 28th.

Destiny dates

Positive: 16

Negative: 3, 5, 7, 8, 12, 13, 14, 15, 24, 25, 26, 27

Mixed: 9, 10, 11, 17, 18, 19, 20, 21, 22, 23

APRIL

Highlights of the month

Although you crave excitement this month, Mars and Saturn will not make it easy for you to enjoy the social invitations offered. You do, however, have a high level of energy and self-confidence, so it's important to assert yourself but please be careful this doesn't create a backlash from those with whom you live and work. These influences are strong around the 1st and 2nd.

Your health and vitality are very strong during the month of April, and in particular during the period of the 3rd and 4th, so finding the time to express your physical needs is vital. It's time to sign up to the gym or at least get out with a friend and start doing some early morning walking. This will further help you with the tough aspect of Mars and Saturn, because rather than bottling up your emotions and creating greater frustration for yourself, the better alternative would be to use the energy from them to improve your health and make your body look better.

Your romantic ideals are very powerful this month and from the 5th you will find yourself living in a world of fantasy, dreaming about your perfect lover. This is okay, unless of course you are already in a relationship, and this might therefore cause a gap between the reality of your current relationship and what you dream about having.

The additional influence of Neptune on you also creates an enhanced level of creativity due to your imagination being very strong. I suggest that you try to direct these powerful forces into activities that will generate contentment rather than a sense of lack.

You just have to accept that April is a time of additional responsibilities and with this is an impressive opportunity for you to exercise unconditional love in all of your relationships. If you can do this you'll grow spiritually and develop a greater sense of inner fulfilment. Particularly after the 22nd, you will have to give much more than you receive and this will also relate to the need for you to serve someone who is not well or struggling with some aspect of their financial life. You can step up to the plate and be a true friend to them.

In the last week of the month you will accomplish an enormous amount in your work but this could get some of your co-workers offside. Your standards will be very high and others will not be able to meet your demands. If you're not much of a team player, this is the time to change that and prove you can be one of the boys or girls.

There is also an opportunity to gain additional money through some speculative enterprise. It's not a bad idea to gamble your way into some extra cash, but I would advise you paper trade on the stock market and study the way commodities rise and fall. Doing so could become a new interest for you at this time.

Romance and friendship

On the 2nd you may be surprised at the behaviour of someone whom you thought much better of. Their actions on the will leave you second-guessing their next moves. If this has been a romantic association, you may lose all feeling for them and

SCORPIO

decide it wasn't worth it after all. On to greener pastures, I guess.

Delays may be necessary between the 5th and the 10th and if this has to do with a love affair it may leave you feeling a little down in the dumps. But you must realise that sometimes a postponement is necessary to regroup your energy and this will in fact turn out better in the long run, giving all concerned time to re-evaluate the benefits of the relationship.

Turning a blind eye to a problem is no way to deal with relationships on the 15th. Something has to be done about the circumstances you are in but you may be confused as to the proper course of action. A third party who may not be directly involved in this issue has some valuable information. Who is that?

A new love affair or at least a friendship can be started sometime around the 20th and it will blossom into something special over the coming months. For those romantically attached, this is an opportunity to revive your love.

If you're feeling bored around the 25th to the 27th, you may end up resorting to over-eating and over-drinking, which over the coming couple of days will make you feel regretful. It's best to get out and have a walk rather than sitting around moping. This will air out your head and also make you feel physically much better. Speaking of health, a loved one will require your services to help them with some medical issue.

Work and money

During the period of the 2nd to the 5th your emotions are deep and obsessive and no one is going to be able to lift you out of this mood. It's best to work alone to sort out this stuff. An emotional purge is not a bad idea.

Imagining the what, why, where and how of your working circumstances is your key focus on the 9th. Imagination, however, is no substitute for determined willpower and well-directed action. You must put your thoughts and dreams into motion now to make your ambitions a reality.

Around the 13th you will suddenly have to make financial adjustments after realising that someone is short of cash and you have to cough up on their behalf. Try to avoid this embarrassing situation beforehand. You will know who this is because they have made a habit of doing it in the past.

You have a choice: you can either cram your studies into a short period, or relax and take longer to finish the degree or course you have in mind. Between the 25th and the 28th your decision will be a distinct benefit to you, freeing your time considerably.

Destiny dates

Positive: 20, 22, 28

Negative: 1, 2, 3, 4, 6, 7, 8, 10, 13, 15

Mixed: 5, 9, 25, 26, 27

MAY

Highlights of the month

With Mercury spotlighting your most intimate and sexual affairs this month, the period of the 2nd till the 5th will bring major transformations in your relationships. This will have a bearing on the way you express your love to your partner and vice versa. This might be a challenge for you, however, especially with the continuing association of Venus and Mars.

Playfulness is the key to all of this. Don't be too serious about inflicting your views and your needs on your partner. And, if they are doing the same, keep it light and breezy. The main point is to have fun in your relationships and learn through your interactions.

Incidentally there will be some unexpected twists and turns in your relationship this month, especially on the 7th when Mercury does an about-face and asks you to question some of the statements of your partner and some of your own belief systems surrounding your marriage or most important friendships.

The full Moon on the 9th is important in that it highlights your own ego and what will be revealed to you can be frightening if you are not prepared to see yourself in an objective way. This is a time to learn more about yourself and to start playing the victim if you are feeling downtrodden and not as successful as you would like.

This is about re-empowering yourself so that you can achieve the things you truly deserve. If you have been spending huge amount of time moping about because you're not achieving the sexual or emotional satisfaction you desire in your relationships, you will have to seriously make some changes.

After the 15th there are excellent opportunities for your business partnerships to thrive. If you're not an independent operator then you can still look forward to some wonderful results from clients and other third parties who will be more than satisfied with the level of service you have been providing them. Not that you are looking for accolades but I can honestly say your employers will be very pleased with the level of professionalism you are exhibiting in your work.

Saturn moves into forward motion on the 17th and it could be a time where you need to accept the inevitable. If you haven't been successful in achieving a pay rise or promotion, you may need to bide your time until the stars are more favourable. Hard work is the secret of getting through this cycle successfully.

Romance and friendship

On the 4th you could be sitting on the fence with respect to a love affair. The practicalities of a relationship are sometimes considerably more complex than simply feeling the feeling. A person you're entangled with now may be too complex by nature and will not fit into the everyday box of conventionality. Many compromises will be necessary.

So what if someone is fickle and all over the place? Does this mean you have to follow suit? Stop trying to keep up and impress by appearing to be the same as others. Be your own person on the 9th, stand your ground morally and forge your

SCORPIO

own destiny. When you get to know a certain person in question, you'll realise just how shallow they are.

Divided loyalties and a conflict of interests will be looming over you between the 17th and the 22nd. Should you direct your energies to a family member or look after a friend who needs your attention as well? A delicate balance is required between both sets of circumstances and unfortunately you may not be able to please both fully.

You will step out of character on the 24th and try to force your opinion on someone whom you know is just not getting it. You run the risk of alienating them and wearing yourself out in the process. You may simply have to be a spectator and watch their destiny unfold.

Your passions run hot between the 28th and the 30th but your peer group may not approve of a person you have feelings for. Nothing may have been said overtly but you have a deep sense that there is a lack of acceptance by them. Remember, this is your life and you must live it on your terms.

Work and money

You have to spend money to make money on the 6th and if you are worried about your security to such an extent that you don't take the odd gamble, your financial status will always remain the same. There are opportunities you should investigate so cast aside your fears.

From the 16th to the 25th you'll be seduced into a new business partnership and can create something for long term through your commercial contacts. If you happen to be a salesperson or representative for your company this is an excellent period that will remunerate you well.

Silly mistakes are the result of lack of sleep and poor concentration. This can be overcome through adjustments in your day-to-day routine. You can't party hard and expect your mind to be quite as sharp as it normally is, can you? A little meditation coupled with sensible exercise is just what the doctor ordered. You can improve matters between the 27th and 29th.

Around the 31st your work plans could be influenced perhaps even disrupted by external factors way out of your control. Health matters or a debt is time-consuming and requires changes. Have Plan B in place before this takes you by surprise.

Destiny dates

Positive: 2, 3, 5, 6, 15, 16, 23, 25, 27

Negative: 7, 30, 31

Mixed: 4, 9, 17, 18, 19, 20, 21, 22, 24, 28, 29

JUNE

Highlights of the month

Watch your tongue this month as it will be easy for you to fly off the handle. One of your ruling planets, Mars, is in full swing in your zone of marriage and relationships. Coupled with the involvement of Mercury you'll be trying to prove yourself verbally and may steamroll others in your effort to be right. You also mustn't allow your excitement to override your emotional balance, particularly in the first couple of days of the month.

On the 2nd it's not a bad idea to have a plan mapped out for the day—no, preferably for the month—as you are likely to do a lot of running around without any tangible results. Have a game plan and clear outcomes both for yourself and others with whom you have meetings. It would be a shame between the 3rd and 6th not to use the powerfully lucky vibrations of Venus and Jupiter to bring you the rewards that are certainly justified.

When Venus enters your zone of partnerships, love will definitely be in the air. You'll be very attractive and also be in a position to capitalise on your meeting with other attractive members of the opposite sex. For many Scorpios this could be the start of an important relationship. Mr or Ms Right may just happen to walk through your front door and this is likely after the 6th, so be prepared.

By the 9th your sex will appeal will reach an all-time peak due to the influence of Pluto. This is one of those periods where it almost impossible to keep your mind on the job. That special person's image will be indelibly implanted on your mind and it will be extremely hard to focus on anything but them.

You will again need to confront several issues on the home front after the 15th when Jupiter focuses your energies on family matters. A deal will be broken or contracts associated with real estate could be in a tailspin. The critical thing to remember here is to be specific about the fine print. Don't let others talk you into doing a deal on a handshake.

These issues will be strongly highlighted up until the 23rd and at this time the Sun will create some legal or bureaucratic problems for you. Dealing with unruly government departments and bureaucrats around the 25th will be particularly annoying.

Around the 30th you could change your professional direction—and just when you thought you had come to a firm decision. This is not a bad thing but will cause you to have second thoughts.

Romance and friendship

A little extra sensitivity will go a long way to help heal past emotional wounds on the 2nd. A family member is being selfish and you may be overreacting to this. A softer and more diplomatic approach is likely to calm the storm. You'll eventually realise that some people are just never going to change their ways.

Don't be half-hearted in making a statement on the 7th. Even if you run the risk of offending someone with the truth it will work out better for you in the long run. Someone else may

SCORPIO

be trying to outdo you on the 8th and you need to seen to be strong among your peers or employers. Truth will just have take precedence over compassion.

A friend's actions could come out of left of field on the 13th and surprise and shock you at the same time. For your own good you may have to sever the relationship at this time before this gets out of hand. Be decisive on this point even if it is a little difficult emotionally. You'll soon realise that you have made the right decision.

Remember that if a person offers you a favour without an apparent expectation of anything in return on the 18th, it's a very rare occurrence. Even if they pretend not to want anything from you, they probably do. You should despise the free lunch and look a little more deeply into the person's motivations. It could come back to bite you.

Between the 22nd and the 26th you may hear news of a wedding or at least some development in the romantic affairs of a very good friend. This will be a surprise but it will be pleasing to your ear. If unmarried yourself, you'll have to admit that you are just a tad envious.

Work and money

On the 2nd and 3rd there's no point being shy and if you need to speak to a mentor or teacher this is the time to do it. Get your point across. If you have to make a presentation, these are the dates on which you'll shine.

Finances are tight but by the 7th your creative communication will secure a new deal that ultimately lifts your earning capacity. A part-time position will pay you a better hourly rate than you expect. On the 18th a subject that has been difficult becomes understandable.

You can expect admiration from co-workers on the 24th but will not quite know how to deal with it. This is not the time for being bashful. Accept respect and admiration for a job well done if it comes your way just now.

Saturn denotes that a serious head-down, rear-up approach is needed to achieve some of your short- and medium-term goals. On the 26th, forget about being seen to be too serious. Who cares if others think you should be different? You're on target and that's what counts.

On the 30th your words must be carefully measured before you make a commitment.

Destiny dates

Positive: 3, 7, 9, 26

Negative: 8, 13, 15, 16, 17, 19, 20, 21

Mixed: 2, 18, 22, 23, 24, 25, 30

JULY

Highlights of the month

You'll continue to be totally uncompromising throughout the month of July because you realise that time is of the essence. Friends and relatives will find it difficult to deal with you but you won't care because you appreciate that to achieve fulfilment in your life you sometimes have to be a little ruthless.

These inflexible attitudes don't always work, however, especially if your choice of friends is not correct. After the 2nd Venus and Neptune indicate that you are likely to meet someone who is not exactly what you first imagined. Your judgement of character is a little impaired. Listen to what your friends say if they have advice to give you about someone. They will probably be pretty close to the mark. Get your ego out of the way and act upon their suggestions.

Between the 9th and the 11th a new work project is likely to get the thumbs up. This will advance your career ambitions and make you more respectable among your peers. In this context it's also not a bad idea to listen to their suggestions and keep trying to work in a team spirit.

This is also a time when you can show your partner that you care about their work endeavours as well. Sharing your fortunes will be a source of happiness to both of you during this cycle. Consequently you'll find that both of you are prepared to make a greater commitment to each other.

There are meetings forecast with people who can benefit your career, and several gatherings with colleagues in a social setting will help catapult your achievements to the next level. Be mindful of the fact that others will talk about you in a not so flattering way due to their jealousy. Try to stay as cool as you can and, between the 12th and 14th, keep your cards close to your chest. You can expect this period to be quite competitive; but don't worry, because Venus constructively assists you once again in easily winning out against your adversaries.

A lunar eclipse takes place in your zone of communications this month and up until the 22nd you'll have to postpone some of your usual pleasures in lieu of tightening up business and financial matters. You'll need to be more forceful in demanding clarity from others. Someone will be trying to pull the wool over your eyes but this is likely to happen only if you're not paying strict attention. Awareness is one of your key words this month.

Romance and friendship

Although a journey or outing on the 6th is disappointing in the end, you will learn about someone through the experience that will be valuable. Experiences in life whether bitter or sweet are ultimately the basis of all wisdom. Be thankful.

Around the 15th you'll receive a letter or e-mail that is useful to your social standing. Use this knowledge wisely, even if it isn't to your own advantage. If you receive free tickets for a concert or an invitation to attend an unusual function, you may have a difficult decision choosing which friend to take along. Between the 18th and the 22nd a secret wish could be fulfilled. The powers of your desire and creative visualisation have now come together and your karma is ripe. The issues of relationship, love and romance are strong and this

SCORPIO

longing may relate to these areas of your life. Good fortune is overdue.

An entertaining situation bring you more than meets the eye on the 24th and 25th. This could be an introduction to someone who has a business proposition or who is able to open doors for you. Be prepared for fun and financial windfalls.

You could be called upon to offer advice between friends who are not seeing eye to eye on the 28th. You'll need to be careful not to appear to be taking sides. This may also relate to members of your own family and, if you think about it, the reason for the rift is quite silly. Don't get involved.

You are fully aware that the past, although not particularly good, has shaped you for the better and you are now in a position to move forward and make life better for yourself. Your luck is changing so keep looking forwards not backwards. You can have some important insights on the 30th.

Work and money

Business arrangements on the 7th should be dealt with in a formal manner. A handshake won't be adequate and you would be foolish to think so. Make sure everyone signs on the dotted line before agreeing.

To remove a thorn you can use another thorn but then both thorns have to be discarded. Your professional life is like this on the 11th. You may have to use an unpleasant situation temporarily to get you out of a fix. It's then up to you to remove both of these circumstances from your life.

The rules in your workplace are changing and this means your job description and possibly even the money you earn could be in question around the 18th and 19th. If you're nervous about this it's imperative you to speak up and resolve this issue. A business meeting over this matter will clarify things.

If you happen to win something or receive a gift on the 22nd you could realise that there is some sort of obligation attached to it. If a gift is offered, read between the lines and make sure that this is not a subtle way of manipulating you. As the old saying goes, 'Despise the free lunch'.

Destiny dates

Positive: 9, 10, 15, 18, 20, 21, 25, 30

Negative: 7, 12, 13, 14, 18

Mixed: 2, 6, 11, 19, 22, 24, 28

AUGUST

Highlights of the month

Your efforts are likely to pay off handsomely this month with the new Moon of the 20th bringing you several fantastic opportunities professionally. If you've made a point of sending out your résumé to the right people at the right time, you're likely to find yourself invited to several interviews to take things to the next level.

Leading up to this date, it's important that, particularly between the 6th and the 12th, you clear the decks so that your mind is not distracted and you are able to answer any questions thrown at you. Looking at your financial situation will no doubt occupy much of your time, which it should. On the 14th and 15th a discovery could surprise you but fortunately it is not too late to make the appropriate adjustments so that things don't get out of hand economically.

Short trips for the purpose of improving your standard of living, increasing your wealth and generally tying up loose ends associated with taxation and other work-related costs are likely after the 16th. Once you clear the air of these issues you will feel refreshed and on target once again.

Some great news can be expected around the 18th when Mercury, the messenger of the gods, delivers important infor-

2009: AUGUST

mation you've been waiting on. You must balance the good news with a few other repercussions because success often demands a sacrifice and this could be one of those occasions. I feel that if you take a new position you will need to travel a little more and make some additional concessions, which could erode your personal time. Hopefully you have the support of your family and loved ones in this unique transitional period.

Mars and Neptune are further enhancing your good fortune during this period and up till the 22nd you'll feel a surge of unparalleled energy in which your dreams can finally come true. Around this time, however, you will feel a little cooler in your emotional responses to your loved ones. This is to be expected as your excitement and focus is wholly and solely on your work and financial commitments. Don't forget to continue to include those who have supported you along the way.

A time of celebration is stirring between the 23rd and the 26th. The Sun activates your zone of friendships, clubs, and group activities. You feel inspired to share your good fortune and your ideas with as many people as you can. Friends and strangers alike will be fascinated by your story. You will not even realise during this period of your life that your words will have greater impact and can even transform the lives of others.

Romance and friendship

An expense in your family may be lessened through an offer of a relative or friend around the 6th. You will feel embarrassed accepting their money but they will generously want to assist so don't slap a gift horse in the mouth.

Your family may be imposing their views upon you around the 9th and you will feel smothered. If out of a sense of obligation you are trying to please them, in the end you won't please yourself. Formulate a new plan for your life that doesn't include them.

SCORPIO

A heated discussion will be resolved on the 15th so don't carry ill-feelings into the future. You must look at differences as positives to help your relationships grow and evolve. Over the coming weeks don't take your partner or spouse's comments too personally or any more seriously.

Your mind will be thinking of distant places, friends and relatives between the 16th and 20th. Your need is to get away but money and expenses may be such that you have to postpone this desire to a more realistic time frame. Your patience will ultimately pay dividends, so don't worry.

You may be blocked in finding a new place to live if house hunting is on your agenda by the 21st. You mustn't leave any stone unturned nor should your personal presentation be lacking in any way whatsoever. Luck has to be enhanced through personal appearance to make the right impact on others.

The health of someone you know could be a concern for you between the 22nd and the 23rd. In your social life, try to avoid situations that you sense could get rowdy or even dangerous on the 28th. You may be embroiled in a clash or a rather uncomfortable scenario.

Work and money

Don't overload yourself on the 10th because it's far better to take a short break and come back refreshed to the job at hand rather than running yourself into the ground.

You have a friend's assistance available to you on the 13th but your pride may not be amenable to asking for their help. Stop being silly and use this opportunity to tie up loose ends.

As long as you're worried about what people feel you won't attempt anything creative on the 20th. You may not be the world's best painter or musician but it's not about creating works of art that are going to revolutionise society. It is all

2009: AUGUST

about self-expression and spiritual growth. Take the time to explore what means are available to better yourself.

The work you are doing is not matched by the amount of money you are earning. You're probably fuming about this and keeping a lid on it. This is not going to help you remedy the situation. Between the 22nd and the 27th speak up and let your feelings be known to higher ups. You could use some extra cash for those expenses, so this is the time to say your bit.

Destiny dates

Positive: 7, 8, 9, 11, 12, 14

Negative: 21

Mixed: 6, 10, 13, 15, 16, 17, 18, 19, 20, 22, 23, 24, 25, 26, 27

SEPTEMBER

Highlights of the month

You have to keep transforming your relationships constantly this year and this will be even more important throughout the month of September. Saturn will make its last ditch attempt to make sure you have learned the lessons it has to teach you about friendship and your most significant intimate relationships.

One area I haven't mentioned to you has to do with your brothers and sisters. If you do have siblings, this transit of Saturn will be particularly powerful in either cementing or tearing down your relationship with them. Longstanding grudges and problems you will have had with them need to be finally resolved if you are to reconnect and grow your love with them in the future.

With your professional activities settling in to a good groove, you can redirect your thoughts to these issues I am now discussing. After the 7th try to express your deepest feelings as openly as you can and don't be afraid to bring out the hidden parts of your relationships; those aspects you've tried so hard to bury for so many years. It will be tough to reveal how you truly feel about another and equally difficult for you to listen to their gripes; but by doing so, a whole new cycle

2009: SEPTEMBER

in your life is about to begin and you want to advance with a clear conscience.

You can foster relationships of unusual nature between the 18th and the 22nd. Visiting places you ordinarily wouldn't consider, taking a punt on an online dating agency, or simply accepting an offer for a blind date are all different avenues that will surprisingly bring you romantic satisfaction in September.

After the 23rd you will be dealing with an abuse of power in some aspect of your life. You will have an insight into how someone has become corrupted by their affluence or position within your place of work or in the life of one of your friends. Your responsibility to do something about this is certain but you will not quite know how to go about it. This will also be a challenge for you but well worth taking up the fight.

After the 25th you have an opportunity to take a short break to re-evaluate the year to date. Spending time alone is not a bad idea to recharge your batteries and also get your head around some of these other issues, especially if you've reached a dead end. Sharing some of this sensitive information with others will also bring into question how much you trust them if you wish to offer this information to them in confidence.

Romance and friendship

You have a full dose of planetary energy between the 2nd and the 6th! Power, health, happiness and wonderful communication will be yours all at once and you will feel invincible. However, don't forget to listen to what others are saying, as you could get caught up in your own joy.

On the 12th an old flame from the past reappears, much to your surprise. If the circumstances are not right and you are in the company of others, this could be awkward or stressful. Try to short-circuit what could be an uncomfortable moment or two beforehand.

SCORPIO

Choices, choices. You will be inundated with many social opportunities between the 18th and the 22nd. You need to choose carefully and make sure that you gain maximum benefits from the events you decide to attend. It may be a good idea to use the pre-emptive approach and qualify which friends are on the bottom of your list. Tell them not to bother sending you an invite.

Do you suffer some phobia, even ever so slightly? You need to do something about this and reclaim your power around the 28th. Usually this has some connection with a childhood trauma or someone in your early family life who triggered these fears. Take a long, hard and honest look at what is causing this and deal with it. If you can't handle it alone, get some professional advice.

If you're finding it hard to speak about a certain matter, the alternative is to write about it. Put pen to paper on the 30th and express how you're feeling, whether good or bad. The important thing about this is that there is no ambiguity about what's being said. Once you've done this, the person you're aiming these thoughts at has no alternative but to consider your viewpoint.

Work and money

Continue to channel the energies of Neptune as it inspires you during this very important transition of your life. You also have the blessing of Venus, which influences your career life, especially around the 14th.

Between the 5th and the 8th your diligence and perseverance will pay off in your work and the combined influence of Mars and Saturn will be a blessing for you. An additional workload and revamped deadlines may well add more pressure to you but you will be in the perfect position to make the most of this.

2009: SEPTEMBER

Your charm plus inspiration equals success and considerable self-satisfaction on the 15th. Try to be clear on your objectives and don't be too unrealistic about forthcoming plans.

Hang in there and you'll see that this has all been worth it. You're becoming tougher now and this can only serve you well in your push for greater success in the coming months.

The period of the 12th to the 20th should be all business, facts and figures, particularly if you're working in a customer service role. You may have several cantankerous clients who are pushing your buttons now and it's up to you to handle them as professionally as possible.

Destiny dates

Positive: 2, 3, 4, 5, 6, 8, 21, 22, 25

Negative: 13, 16, 17, 23

Mixed: 7, 12, 14, 15, 18, 19, 20, 28, 30

OCTOBER

Highlights of the month

For those of you who are parents, the period of October will be one in which you can take a great deal more pride in your children. Part of your temperament will soften throughout the first couple of weeks of the month and, if responsibility has been an overwhelming part of your life, you'll now be able to sit back, relax and truly enjoy some of the things you have worked hard for.

Between the 1st and the 10th, you will find yourself among younger kids, not just your own; but in your meetings with others generally it's likely that a youthful energy will pervade your social life. This will in turn make you also feel younger and more exuberant in all your activities.

Uranus, the planet of excitement and unpredictability, has an important part to play in your romantic activities this month, especially between the 11th and the 15th when Venus enters into your sphere of influence. Expect the unexpected! Your meetings with members of the opposite sex will be anything but dull and will in fact challenge you to step outside your usual conservative behaviour. You'll be tempted to try something different and explore what I refer to as the science of human possibilities.

Outstanding issues on the home front are finally cleared up once and for all and those of you who will have had delays with the bank or mortgage loans will be pleased to note that after the 13th it's all systems go once again.

If you have a desire to prove your leadership skills then this month you can do so. People will be looking to you for direction and it's up to you to set the example. Homemakers and those who are not actively engaged in a career per se can still offer their services and leadership skills to those who call upon them to help. There's a subtle aspect to this reclaiming of power and, if you've not been respected by family members, change is likely to take place by laying down the law and demanding that others treat you as an equal.

Scorpio, October and November are the most powerful months of the year when the Sun returns to its natal position. The sign of Scorpio is activated by the solar rays and this is usually a lucky period when your personality will shine and generally all areas of your life will prosper. This occurs around the 23rd or 24th. Make it a point to give yourself time to enjoy your own company and of those you love.

Romance and friendship

Are you being left out of social engagements? Do your friends seem a little subversive or cagey? On the 8th you need to get to the bottom of some unusual behaviour in your group and you should trust your intuition that all is not well. It may be time to make some changes in the area of your friendships.

On the 14th a fortunate event is of no use if you are not aware that it is happening. Keep your ears and eyes wide open because something magical can occur in your relationships. If you've been on the lookout for that special person, this cycle could well be an important turning point for you in love.

If things haven't been going so well in your romantic life, try to think back to those feelings and experiences that

SCORPIO

gave you a rush of love and excitement. Between the 18th and the 23rd you need to regenerate these emotions rather than brooding on the negative aspects of what is happening. When you look at the cup, is it the half empty or half full?

You can mediate between family members who are squabbling and bring peace to the family home on the 25th. You mustn't appear to take sides even though you secretly do favour one person over the other. Your lesson in life now is to remain impartial and exercise balanced judgement within a rather turbulent set of circumstances.

Your love life will suddenly take a turn for the better 28th and 30th. An unexpected meeting, a call from someone you've recently met or an invitation to a social function will prove to be fortuitous. Venus and the Moon bless you with ample opportunities so the only problem I see for you just now is the matter of choices and ... more choices.

Work and money

The influence of Mars will cause you to feel extremely active in your working life, particularly after the 8th. This means you can achieve anything you want just by focusing the direction you want. Bring your attention to worthwhile matters.

Your ruling planets are in good form so don't worry too much about the current state of financial affairs. Everything will come out all right between the 10th and the 14th. The pressure you're feeling at work will also subside by the new Moon of the 18th. Give it all you've got.

You will be more unconventional than usual on the 28th and this will appear out of character to others. You mustn't push your new ideas too forcefully before explaining the end result. By giving people the bigger picture you are more likely to gain their support.

2009: OCTOBER

After the 29th it's not a good idea to commit yourself to those larger purchases just because you are expecting additional bonuses or extra cash. These lump sums you anticipate may be held up for some reason or other and you will find yourself out on a limb. Spend only the money you can see and feel.

Destiny dates

Positive: 1, 2, 3, 4, 5, 6, 7, 9, 10, 11, 12, 13, 15, 24, 30

Negative: 18, 19, 20, 21, 22, 25

Mixed: 8, 14, 23, 28, 29

NOVEMBER

Highlights of the month

The month commences on a work note with some concerns about deadlines and whether or not you can finish your tasks on time. Don't worry, the full Moon on the 2nd brings with it some interesting observations and revelations on your part, which help you attack your work from a completely lateral point of view. You will achieve a considerable amount and at the 11th hour will be surprised when someone who has finished their work early offers you a hand due to their own boredom.

November is also to be highly prized as one of your best months due to the motion of Mars at the zenith of your horoscope. Simply put, it means you are able to make great strides professionally and you'll be popular and successful at every step of your journey this month.

By the 8th your personal charm also kicks in to lend a helping hand due to Mars, so you won't need to beg others to get their help. A simple smile or a nod will suffice for them to do your bidding. Isn't it nice to not have to struggle or argue about getting things done, especially if you've been the one taking out the garbage, mowing the lawns and generally doing every single chore around the house? Your family will be prepared to pull their weight now and this will cause you to breathe a sigh of relief.

You are proactive not only professionally but in your personal life during this period. Don't be too forceful in demanding what you think is rightfully yours emotionally around the 18th as it could have some ramifications you hadn't planned on. Others who are in your company at this time could perceive your behaviour as less than socially acceptable, or culturally uncomfortable, or out of place.

You might want to tell them all to go hell so that you can live your life on your terms but you'll have to pay a price for this once the alcohol has worn off. Don't forget the morning after will arrive and could do so with you feeling a great deal of regret for being too forthright.

Saturn is not all doom and gloom and this month is a case in point when it begins to influence your expenses and debts. Between the 20th and the 30th you will naturally feel less inclined to fritter away your money from this point forward and can start to see some real increase in savings. It's time to look at growing your nest egg and securing your future financial security.

Romance and friendship

You are all fired up on the 4th but may inadvertently pick on the wrong person if it's a mental challenge you desire. They may be just as motivated to win an argument and this could end up being stressful rather than playful. Get out, have a run or go to the gym rather than building up nervous energy now. You don't need any additional problems, so make peace.

Your advances to a friend may not be appreciated on the 11th, even though you feel as if you have read their signals correctly. Read between the lines more carefully before opening your heart to them. What we perceive is often not the way others perceive the same situation.

SCORPIO

Someone you consider a good friend or possibly even your romantic partner might finally decide that it is time for a major life change between the 16th and the 22nd. This may come from left of field and surprise you. You may have to make adjustments to their new plans.

After the 27th personal differences with a friend can finally be resolved and, even though you may accept that you are not destined to be the best of buddies any more, you can still respect each other for these differences. It's time to move on and enlarge your circle of friends and acquaintances. This Christmas and new year is an excellent cycle to look forwards, not backwards.

Although your love life has been on the backburner you can still socialise and have a laugh around the 29th when your charisma will be very strong. You're also intense about improving your grades and will make some arrangements for coaching or joint study with a friend. This will bring positive results very soon.

Your sexual energies are strong on the 30th.

Work and money

The spotlight will be on financial matters but not necessarily in a bad way on the 5th. If you've been building your nest egg there could be additional opportunities to enhance your earning capacity.

You can dominate your professional circle between the 8th and the 12th. Educationally, this too can be a wonderful period to achieve great goals. Your power will be magnified and you're able to receive the help you need to do even bigger and better things. Business becomes busier due to Mars.

Between the 13th and the 19th you will find yourself embroiled in dealing with money that is owed to you or debts that you haven't serviced effectively. You'd prefer to be on top of all of this stuff so it's important that you get clarity on any agreements or contracts.

As your ruling planet continues its powerful motion, you could be feeling intense and overly emotional about work matters. Power plays are likely between the 27th and the 29th so you need to be on your own best behaviour to avoid confrontational run-ins. Keeping yourself on the move and out of other people's faces is the best approach.

Destiny dates

Positive: 2, 5, 8, 9, 10, 12, 23, 24, 25, 26, 30

Negative: 4, 13, 14, 15

Mixed: 11, 16, 17, 18, 19, 20, 21, 22, 27, 28, 29

DECEMBER

Highlights of the month

The fortunate planets Jupiter and Neptune endow you with a clearer insight into who you are and what you should be doing in life. This is probably one of the most important realisations for you in 2009. A deeper understanding of your personal relationships and where you fit into the scheme of your professional life and the ambitions you want to realise are all part of this important culmination in the last month of the year.

Somehow you'll attract excellent characters into your life that can be of service and inspiration on your path. Around the 3rd you will find that the most casual remark draws attention in a positive way from those who see something special in you. You mustn't be too humble or you will miss an opportunity to further your aspirations. You can share your wisdom without fear.

Deep and careful thinking will pay handsome dividends as the year draws to a close. Think before you speak and if in doubt postpone that call or message until you are clear on what direction you wish to take. Someone will hurt you at this time and you'll have to think about the consequences of retaliating too impulsively.

2009: DECEMBER

Some decisions this year will be difficult because you realise that you can't afford to spend any further time with those who are not as passionate about life as you. You must be with people who can share your vision, your love and intensity, which are all true Scorpio character traits. Leading up to Christmas and in particular around the 22nd, a journey will act as a catalyst in this respect. You will meet someone perhaps from afar who can meet these new standards and fulfil your needs.

You mustn't feel guilty that you are taking a different path now even in the face of criticism from those in whom you trust and believe. Sooner or later you must tread a path that is of your own making and this is based upon courage and earnestness.

Venus brings you great happiness between the 23rd and the 26th so Christmas should indeed be a time of great happiness for you this year, as long as you are prepared to live by your own principles. And the cherry on top of the cake in December must surely be Mars traversing your career zone and the additional power of Venus, the Sun and Mercury in your income zone. This final month of 2009 should bring you immense of satisfaction and confidence that 2010 will begin with a bang.

Relax now. There's no need to rush any decision. Simply enjoy the holiday season and reminisce on the successes of this year.

Romance and friendship

You can call on help to get you through a difficult period from the 4th to the 7th and will be amazed at the amount of support you can muster just when you thought friends had deserted you. You may not need to ask for assistance because someone close will sense your need. They do say that many hands make light work so don't worry, you will get through this problem.

SCORPIO

Your spiritual energies are likely to be quite pronounced after the 9th. You are recognising the deeper aspects of human kindness and will feel that the commercialisation of this special time is rather off-putting. Be yourself and share the spirit of Christmas without feeling obliged to part with a lot of money.

You have the travel bug around the 16th and so it's not a bad idea to kick off Christmas with a trip away from home. You're emotional about these issues as well and it's likely that your relationship with a friend or lover will have a bearing on this journey.

Sort out family problems before you leave as this could continue to be an issue in the coming new year. A telephone call on the 17th will smooth things over.

Your mind could feel like a revolving door over some unpleasant event in the past on the 24th. If you bump into someone who was part of this unsavoury experience it will be even harder. Before committing to a party or get-together, find out whether or not that individual will be present and if so choose an alternative gig.

You have some unfinished emotional business to deal with on the 31st so it's best to face the music. Once you say your piece and the other person has a chance to get things off their chest, you can move forward confidently into the new year.

Work and money

You must continue to get clarification on contractual agreements and obligations, even if they are only verbal. On the 5th you may give the go-ahead to someone to do something only to find that they have misled you or taken advantage of your goodwill. You've only got yourself to blame if you end up being used like this. More attention to detail is necessary.

2009: DECEMBER

Friends and co-workers appear a little distant on the 10th and the 11th but you mustn't let this be a reflection on the goodwill between you. Surely you understand that this is the time of madness, you know, Christmas and all. Everyone is so caught up in what they're doing that they may be overlooking you but only for the time being. Don't be too preoccupied with these negative thoughts.

It may be unavoidable but an important business or financial matter may need to be discussed over the telephone on the 16th. If the person is reluctant to do so, you may be in a spot of bother as you realise catching up with them in person may not be possible. Force the hand and have the discussion whether they like it or not.

Destiny dates

Positive: 3, 4, 6, 7, 9, 22, 23, 25, 26

Negative: 10, 11

Mixed: 5, 16, 24, 31

SCORPIO

2009: Astronumerology

SCORPIO

> *A person with a bad name is already half-hanged.*
>
> —Proverb

The power behind your name

By adding the numbers of your name you can see which planet is ruling you. Each of the letters of the alphabet is assigned a number, which is tabled below. These numbers are ruled by the planets. This is according to the ancient Chaldean system of numerology and is very different to the Pythagorean system to which many refer.

Each number is assigned a planet:

AIQJY	=	1	**Sun**
BKR	=	2	**Moon**
CGLS	=	3	**Jupiter**
DMT	=	4	**Uranus**
EHNX	=	5	**Mercury**
UVW	=	6	**Venus**
OZ	=	7	**Neptune**
FP	=	8	**Saturn**
—	=	9	**Mars**

Notice that the number 9 is not allotted a letter because it is considered special. Once the numbers have been added you will see that a single planet rules your name and personal affairs. Many famous actors, writers and musicians change their names to attract the energy of a luckier planet. You can experiment with the table and try new names or add letters of your second name to see how that vibration suits you. It's a lot of fun!

2009: ASTRONUMEROLOGY

Here is an example of how to find out the power of your name. If your name is John Smith, calculate the ruling planet by correlating each letter to a number in the table like this:

J O H N   S M I T H

1 7 5 5   3 4 1 4 5

Now add the numbers like this:

1 + 7 + 5 + 5 + 3 + 4 + 1 + 4 + 5 = 35

Then add 3 + 5 = 8

The ruling number of John Smith's name is 8, which is ruled by Saturn. Now study the name-number table to reveal the power of your name. The numbers 3 and 5 will also play a secondary role in John's character and destiny so in this case you would also study the effects of Jupiter and Mercury.

Name-number table

Your name number	Ruling planet	Your name characteristics
1	Sun	Charismatic personality. Great vitality and life force. Physically active and outgoing. Attracts good friends and individuals in powerful positions. Good government connections. Intelligent, dramatic, showy and successful. A loyal number for relationships.
2	Moon	Soft, emotional temperament. Changeable moods but psychic, intuitive senses. Imaginative nature and compassionate expression of feelings. Loves family, mother and home life. Night owl who probably needs more sleep.

SCORPIO

		Success with the public and/or the opposite sex.
3	Jupiter	Outgoing, optimistic number with lucky overtones. Attracts opportunities without trying. Good sense of timing. Religious or spiritual aspirations. Can investigate the meaning of life. Loves to travel and explore the world and people.
4	Uranus	Explosive personality with many quirky aspects. Likes the untried and untested. Forward thinking, with many unusual friends. Gets bored easily so needs plenty of stimulating experiences. Innovative, technological and creative. Wilful and stubborn when wants to be. Unexpected events in life may be positive or negative.
5	Mercury	Quick-thinking mind with great powers of speech. Extremely active life; always on the go and lives on nervous energy. Youthful attitude and never grows old. Looks younger than actual age. Young friends and humorous disposition. Loves reading and writing.
6	Venus	Charming personality. Graceful and attractive character, who cherishes friends and social life. Musical or artistic interests. Good for money making as well as numerous love affairs. Career in

2009: ASTRONUMEROLOGY

the public eye is possible. Loves family but is often overly concerned by friends.

7	Neptune	Intuitive, spiritual and self-sacrificing nature. Easily duped by those who need help. Loves to dream of life's possibilities. Has healing powers. Dreams are revealing and prophetic. Loves the water and will have many journeys in life. Spiritual aspirations dominate worldly desires.
8	Saturn	Hard-working, focused individual with slow but certain success. Incredible concentration and self-sacrifice for a goal. Money orientated but generous when trust is gained. Professional but may be a hard taskmaster. Demands highest standards and needs to learn to enjoy life a little more.
9	Mars	Incredible physical drive and ambition. Sports and outdoor activities are keys to health. Combative and likes to work and play just as hard. Protective of family, friends and territory. Individual tastes in life but is also self-absorbed. Needs to listen to others' advice to gain greater success.

SCORPIO

Your 2009 planetary ruler

Astrology and numerology are closely linked. Each planet rules over a number between 1 and 9. Both your name and your birth date are ruled by planetary energies. Here are the planets and their ruling numbers:

1 Sun; 2 Moon; 3 Jupiter; 4 Uranus; 5 Mercury; 6 Venus; 7 Neptune; 8 Saturn; 9 Mars

Simply add the numbers of your birth date and the year in question to find out which planet will control the coming year for you. Here is an example:

If you were born on 12 November, add the numerals 1 and 2 (12, your day of birth) and 1 and 1 (11, your month of birth) to the year in question, in this case 2009 (current year), like this:

Add 1 + 2 + 1 + 1 + 2 + 0 + 0 + 9 = 16

Then add these numbers again: 1 + 6 = 7

The planet ruling your individual karma for 2009 will be Neptune because this planet rules the number 7.

You can even take your ruling name number as shown above and add it to the year in question to throw more light on your coming personal affairs like this:

John Smith = 8

Year coming = 2009

Add 8 + 2 + 0 + 0 + 9 = 19

Add 1 + 9 = 10

Add 1 + 0 = 1

This is the ruling year number using your name number as a basis. Therefore, study the Sun's (number 1) influence for 2009. Enjoy!

1 = Year of the Sun

Overview

The Sun is the brightest object in the heavens and rules number 1 and the sign of Leo. Because of this the coming year will bring you great success and popularity.

You'll be full of life and radiant vibrations and are more than ready to tackle your new nine-year cycle, which begins now. Any new projects you commence are likely to be successful.

Your health and vitality will be very strong and your stamina at its peak. Even if you happen to have the odd problem with your health, your recuperative power will be strong.

You have tremendous magnetism this year so social popularity won't be a problem for you. I see many new friends and lovers coming into your life. Expect loads of invitations to parties and fun-filled outings. Just don't take your health for granted as you're likely to burn the candle at both ends.

With success coming your way, don't let it go to your head. You must maintain humility, which will make you even more popular in the coming year.

Love and pleasure

This is an important cycle for renewing your love and connections with your family, particularly if you have children. The Sun is connected with the sign of Leo and therefore brings an increase in musical and theatrical activities. Entertainment and other creative hobbies will be high on your agenda and bring you a great sense of satisfaction.

Work

You won't have to make too much effort to be successful this year as the brightness of the Sun will draw opportunities to you. Changes in work are likely and if you have been concerned

SCORPIO

that opportunities are few and far between, 2009 will be different. You can expect some sort of promotion or an increase in income because your employers will take special note of your skills and service orientation.

Improving your luck

Leo is the ruler of number 1 and therefore, if you're born under this star sign, 2009 will be particularly lucky. For others, July and August, the months of Leo, will bring good fortune. The 1st, 8th, 15th and 22nd hours of Sundays especially will give you a unique sort of luck in any sort of competition or activities generally. Keep your eye out for those born under Leo as they may be able to contribute something to your life and may even have a karmic connection to you. This is a particularly important year for your destiny.

Your lucky numbers in this coming cycle are 1, 10, 19 and 28.

2 = Year of the Moon

Overview

There's nothing more soothing than the cool light of the full Moon on a clear night. The Moon is emotional and receptive and controls your destiny in 2009. If you're able to use the positive energies of the Moon, it will be a great year in which you can realign and improve your relationships, particularly with family members.

Making a commitment to becoming a better person and bringing your emotions under control will also dominate your thinking. Try not to let your emotions get the better of you throughout the coming year because you may be drawn into the changeable nature of these lunar vibrations as well. If you fail to keep control of your emotional life you'll later regret some of your actions. You must carefully blend thinking with feeling to arrive at the best results. Your luck throughout 2009 will certainly be determined by the state of your mind.

2009: ASTRONUMEROLOGY

Because the Moon and the sign of Cancer rule the number 2 there is a certain amount of change to be expected this year. Keep your feelings steady and don't let your heart rule your head.

Love and pleasure

Your primary concern in 2009 will be your home and family life. You'll be keen to finally take on those renovations, or work on your garden. You may even think of buying a new home. You can at last carry out some of those plans and make your dreams come true. If you find yourself a little more temperamental than usual, do some extra meditation and spend time alone until you sort this out. You mustn't withhold your feelings from your partner as this will only create frustration.

Work

During 2009 your focus will be primarily on feelings and family; however, this doesn't mean you can't make great strides in your work as well. The Moon rules the general public and what you might find is that special opportunities and connections with the world at large present themselves to you. You could be working with large numbers of people.

If you're looking for a better work opportunity, try to focus your attention on women who can give you a hand. Use your intuition as it will be finely tuned this year. Work and career success depends upon your instincts.

Improving your luck

The sign of Cancer is your ruler this year and because the Moon rules Mondays, both this day of the week and the month of July are extremely lucky for you. The 1st, 8th, 15th and 22nd hours on Mondays will be very powerful. Pay special attention to the new and full Moon days throughout 2009.

The numbers 2, 11 and 29 are lucky for you.

3 = Year of Jupiter

Overview

The year 2009 will be a 3 year for you and, because of this, Jupiter and Sagittarius will dominate your affairs. This is very lucky and shows that you'll be motivated to broaden your horizons, gain more money and become extremely popular in your social circles. It looks like 2009 will be a fun-filled year with much excitement.

Jupiter and Sagittarius are generous to a fault and so likewise, your openhandedness will mark the year. You'll be friendly and helpful to all of those around you.

Pisces is also under the rulership of the number 3 and this brings out your spiritual and compassionate nature. You'll become a much better person, reducing your negative karma by increasing your self-awareness and spiritual feelings. You will want to share your luck with those you love.

Love and pleasure

Travel and seeking new adventures will be part and parcel of your romantic life this year. Travelling to distant lands and meeting unusual people will open your heart to fresh possibilities of romance.

You'll try novel and audacious things and will find yourself in a different circle of friends. Compromise will be important in making your existing relationships work. Talk about your feelings. If you are currently in a relationship you'll feel an upswing in your affection for them. This is a perfect opportunity to deepen your love for each other and take your relationship to a new level.

If you're not yet attached to someone just yet, there's good news for you. Great opportunities lie in store for you and a spiritual or karmic connection may be experienced in 2009.

2009: ASTRONUMEROLOGY

Work

Great fortune can be expected through your working life in the next twelve months. Your friends and work colleagues will want to help you achieve your goals. Even your employers will be amenable to your requests for extra money or a better position within the organisation.

If you want to start a new job or possibly begin an independent line of business this is a great year to do it. Jupiter looks set to give you plenty of opportunities, success and a superior reputation.

Improving your luck

As long as you can keep a balanced view of things and not overdo anything, your luck will increase dramatically throughout 2009. The important thing is to remain grounded and not be too airy-fairy about your objectives. Be realistic about your talents and capabilities and don't brag about your skills or achievements. This will only invite envy from others.

Moderate your social life as well and don't drink or eat too much as this will slow your reflexes and lessen your chances for success.

You have plenty of spiritual insights this year so you should use them to their maximum. In the 1st, 8th, 15th and 24th hours of Thursdays you should use your intuition to enhance your luck, and the numbers 3, 12, 21 and 30 are also lucky for you. March and December are your lucky months but generally the whole year should go pretty smoothly for you.

4 = Year of Uranus

Overview

The electric and exciting planet of the zodiac Uranus and its sign of Aquarius rule your affairs throughout 2009. Dramatic events will surprise and at the same time unnerve you in your professional and personal life. So be prepared!

SCORPIO

You'll be able to achieve many things this year and your dreams are likely to come true, but you mustn't be distracted or scattered with your energies. You'll be breaking through your own self-limitations and this will present challenges from your family and friends. You'll want to be independent and develop your spiritual powers and nothing will stop you.

Try to maintain discipline and an orderly lifestyle so you can make the most of these special energies this year. If unexpected things do happen, it's not a bad idea to have an alternative plan so you don't lose momentum.

Work

Technology, computing and the Internet will play a larger role in your professional life this coming year. You'll have to move ahead with the times and learn new skills if you want to achieve success.

A hectic schedule is likely, so make sure your diary is with you at all times. Try to be more efficient and don't waste time.

New friends and alliances at work will help you achieve even greater success in the coming period. Becoming a team player will be even more important towards gaining satisfaction in your professional endeavours.

Love and pleasure

You want something radical, something different in your relationships this year. It's quite likely that your love life will be feeling a little less than exciting so you'll take some important steps to change that. If your partner is as progressive as you'll be this year, then your relationship is likely to improve and fulfil both of you.

In your social life you will meet some very unusual people whom you'll feel are specially connected to you spiritually. You may want to ditch everything for the excitement and passion of a completely new relationship, but tread carefully as this may not work out exactly as you'd expected.

Improving your luck

Moving too quickly and impulsively will cause you problems on all fronts, so be a little more patient and think your decisions through more carefully. Social, romantic and professional opportunities will come to you but take a little time to investigate the ramifications of your actions.

The 1st, 8th, 15th and 20th hours of any Saturday are lucky, but love and luck are likely to cross your path when you least expect it. The numbers 4, 13, 22 and 31 are also lucky for you this year.

5 = Year of Mercury

Overview

The supreme planet of communication, Mercury, is your ruling planet throughout 2009. The number 5, which is connected to Mercury, will confer upon you success through your intellectual abilities.

Any form of writing or speaking will be improved and this will be, to a large extent, underpinning your success. Your imagination will be stimulated by this planet with many incredible new and exciting ideas will come to mind.

Mercury and the number 5 are considered somewhat indecisive. Be firm in your attitude and don't let too many ideas or opportunities distract and confuse you. By all means get as much information as you can to help you make the right decision.

I see you involved with money proposals, job applications, even contracts that need to be signed so remain clear-headed as much as possible.

Your business skills and clear and concise communication will be at the heart of your life in 2009.

SCORPIO

Love and pleasure

Mercury, which rules the signs of Gemini and Virgo, will make your love life a little difficult due to its changeable nature. On the one hand you'll feel passionate and loving to your partner, yet on the other you will feel like giving it all up for the excitement of a new affair. Maintain the middle ground.

Also, try not to be too critical with your friends and family members. The influence of Virgo makes you prone to expecting much more from others than they're capable of giving. Control your sharp tongue and don't hurt people's feelings. Encouraging others is the better path, leading to more emotional satisfaction.

Work

Speed will dominate your professional life in 2009. You'll be flitting from one subject to another and taking on far more than you can handle. You'll need to make some serious changes in your routine to handle the avalanche of work that will come your way. You'll also be travelling with your work, but not necessarily overseas.

If you're in a job you enjoy then this year will give you additional successes. If not, it may be time to move on.

Improving your luck

Communication is the secret of attaining your desires in the coming twelve months. Keep focused on one idea rather than scattering your energies in all directions and your success will be speedier.

By looking after your health, sleeping well and exercising regularly, you'll build up your resilience and mental strength.

The 1st, 8th, 15th and 20th hours of Wednesday are lucky so it's best to schedule your meetings and other important

2009: ASTRONUMEROLOGY

social engagements during these times. The lucky numbers for Mercury are 5, 14, 23 and 32.

6 = Year of Venus

Overview

Because you're ruled by 6 this year, love is in the air! Venus, Taurus and Libra are well known for their affinity with romance, love, and even marriage. If ever you were going to meet a soulmate and feel comfortable in love, 2009 must surely be your year.

Taurus has a strong connection to money and practical affairs as well, so finances will also improve if you are diligent about work and security issues.

The important thing to keep in mind this year is that sharing love and making that important soul connection should be kept high on your agenda. This will be an enjoyable period in your life.

Love and pleasure

Romance is the key thing for you this year and your current relationships will become more fulfilling if you happen to be attached. For singles, a 6 year heralds an important meeting that eventually leads to marriage.

You'll also be interested in fashion, gifts, jewellery and all sorts of socialising. It's at one of these social engagements that you could meet the love of your life. Remain available!

Venus is one of the planets that has a tendency to overdo things, so be moderate in your eating and drinking. Try generally to maintain a modest lifestyle.

Work

You'll have a clearer insight into finances and your future security during a number 6 year. Whereas you may have had

SCORPIO

additional expenses and extra distractions previously, your mind will be more settled and capable of longer-term planning along these lines.

With the extra cash you might see this year, decorating your home or office will give you a special sort of satisfaction.

Social affairs and professional activities will be strongly linked. Any sort of work-related functions may offer you romantic opportunities as well. On the other hand, be careful not to mix up your workplace relationships with romantic ideals. This could complicate some of your professional activities.

Improving your luck

You'll want more money and a life of leisure and ease in 2009. Keep working on your strengths and eliminate your negative personality traits to create greater luck and harmony in your life.

Moderate all your actions and don't focus exclusively on money and material objects. Feed your spiritual needs as well. By balancing the inner and outer you'll see that your romantic and professional life will be enhanced more easily.

The 1st, 8th, 15th and 20th hours on Fridays will be very lucky for you and new opportunities will arise for you at those times. You can use the numbers 6, 15, 24 and 33 to increase luck in your general affairs.

7 = Year of Neptune

Overview

The last and most evolved sign of the zodiac is Pisces, which is ruled by Neptune. The number 7 is deeply connected with this zodiacal sign and governs you in 2009. Your ideals seem to be clearer and more spiritually orientated than ever before. Your desire to evolve and understand your inner self will be a double-edged sword. It depends on how organised you are as to how well you can use these spiritual and abstract concepts in your practical life.

Your past emotional hurts and deep emotional issues will be dealt with and removed for good, if you are serious about becoming a better human being.

Spend a little more time caring for yourself rather than others, as it's likely some of your friends will drain you of energy with their own personal problems. Of course, you mustn't turn a blind eye to the needs of others, but don't ignore your own personal needs in the process.

Love and pleasure

Meeting people with similar life views and spiritual aspirations will rekindle your faith in relationships. If you do choose to develop a new romance, make sure that there is a clear understanding of the responsibilities of one to the other. Don't get swept off your feet by people who have ulterior motives.

Keep your relationships realistic and see that the most idealistic partnerships must eventually come down to Earth. Deal with the practicalities of life.

Work

This is a year of hard work, but one in which you'll come to understand the deeper significance of your professional ideals. You may discover a whole new aspect to your career, which involves a more compassionate and self-sacrificing side to your personality.

You'll also find that your way of working will change and that you'll be more focused and able to get into the spirit of whatever you do. Finding meaningful work is very likely and therefore this could be a year when money, security, creativity and spirituality overlap to bring you a great sense of personal satisfaction.

SCORPIO

Tapping into your greater self through meditation and self-study will bring you great benefits throughout 2009.

Improving your luck

Using self-sacrifice along with discrimination will be an unusual method of improving your luck. The laws of karma state that what you give, you receive in greater measure. This is one of the principal themes for you in 2009.

The 1st, 8th, 15th and 20th hours of Tuesdays are your lucky times. The numbers 7, 16, 25 and 34 should be used to increase your lucky energies.

8 = Year of Saturn

Overview

The earthy and practical sign of Capricorn and its ruler Saturn are intimately linked to the number 8, which rules you in 2009. Your discipline and farsightedness will help you achieve great things in the coming year. With cautious discernment, slowly but surely you will reach your goals.

It may be that due to the influence of the solitary Saturn, your best work and achievement will be behind closed doors away from the limelight. You mustn't fear this as you'll discover many new things about yourself. You'll learn just how strong you really are.

Love and pleasure

Work will overshadow your personal affairs in 2009, but you mustn't let this erode the personal relationships you have. Becoming a workaholic brings great material successes but will also cause you to become too insular and aloof. Your family members won't take too kindly to you working 100-hour weeks.

Responsibility is one of the key words for this number and you will therefore find yourself in a position of authority that

2009: ASTRONUMEROLOGY

leaves very little time for fun. Try to make time to enjoy the company of friends and family and by all means schedule time off on the weekends as it will give you the peace of mind you're looking for.

Because of your responsible attitude it will be very hard for you not to assume a greater role in your workplace and this indicates longer working hours with the likelihood of a promotion with equally good remuneration.

Work

Money is high on your agenda in 2009. Number 8 is a good money number according to the Chinese and this year is at last likely to bring you the fruits of your hard labour. You are cautious and resourceful in all your dealings and will not waste your hard-earned savings. You will also be very conscious of using your time wisely.

You will be given more responsibilities and you're likely to take them on, if only to prove to yourself that you can handle whatever life dishes up.

Expect a promotion in which you will play a leading role in your work. Your diligence and hard work will pay off, literally, in a bigger salary and more respect from others.

Improving your luck

Caution is one of the key characteristics of the number 8 and is linked to Capricorn. But being overly cautious could cause you to miss valuable opportunities. If an offer is put to you, try to think outside the square and balance it with your naturally cautious nature.

Be gentle and kind to yourself. By loving yourself, others will naturally love you, too. The 1st, 8th, 15th and 20th hours of Saturdays are exceptionally lucky for you as are the numbers 1, 8, 17, 26 and 35.

SCORPIO

9 = Year of Mars

Overview

You are now entering the final year of a nine-year cycle dominated by the planet Mars and the sign of Aries. You'll be completing many things and are determined to be successful after several years of intense work.

Some of your relationships may now have reached their use-by date and even these personal affairs may need to be released. Don't let arguments and disagreements get in the road of friendly resolution in these areas of your life.

Mars is a challenging planet and, this year, although you will be very active and productive, you may find others trying to obstruct the achievement of your goals. As a result you may react strongly to them, thereby creating disharmony in your workplace. Don't be so impulsive or reckless, and generally slow things down. The slower, steadier approach has greater merit this year.

Love and pleasure

If you become too bossy and pushy with friends this year you will just end up pushing them out of your life. It's a year to end certain friendships but by the same token it could be the perfect time to end conflicts and thereby bolster your love affairs in 2009.

If you're feeling a little irritable and angry with those you love, try getting rid of these negative feelings through some intense, rigorous sports and physical activity. This will definitely relieve tension and improve your personal life.

Work

Because you're healthy and able to work at a more intense pace you'll achieve an incredible amount in the coming year. Overwork could become a problem if you're not careful.

Because the number 9 and Mars are infused with leadership energy, you'll be asked to take the reins of the job and steer your company or group in a certain direction. This will bring with it added responsibility but also a greater sense of purpose for you.

Improving your luck

Because of the hot and restless energy of the number 9, it is important to create more mental peace in your life this year. Lower the temperature, so to speak, and decompress your relationships rather than becoming aggravated. Try to talk to your work partners and loved ones rather than telling them what to do. This will generally pick up your health and your relationships.

The 1st, 8th, 15th and 20th hours of Tuesdays are the luckiest for you this year and, if you're involved in any disputes or need to attend to health issues, these times are also very good for the best results. Your lucky numbers are 9, 18, 27 and 36.

SCORPIO

2009:
Your Daily Planner

SCORPIO

> *Learn from yesterday, live for today, hope for tomorrow.*
>
> —Anonymous

There is a little-known branch of astrology called electional astrology, and it can help you select the most appropriate times for many of your day-to-day activities.

Ancient astrologers understood the planetary patterns and how they impacted on each of us. This allowed them to suggest the best possible times to start various important activities. Many farmers today still use this approach: they understand the phases of the Moon, and attest to the fact that planting seeds on certain lunar days produces a far better crop than planting on other days.

The following section covers many areas of daily life, and uses the cycles of the Moon and the combined strength of the other planets to work out the best times to start different types of activity.

So to create your own personal almanac, first select the activity you are interested in, and then quickly scan the year for the best months to start it. When you have selected the month, you can finetune your timing by finding the best specific dates. You can then be sure that the planetary energies will be in sync with you, offering you the best possible outcome.

Coupled with what you know about your monthly and weekly trends, the daily planner can be a powerful tool to help you capitalise on opportunities that come your way this year.

Good luck, and may the planets bless you with great success, fortune and happiness in 2009!

Starting activities

How many times have you made a new year's resolution to begin a diet or be a better person in your relationships? And

2009: YOUR DAILY PLANNER

how many times has it not worked out? Well, the reason may be partly that you started out at the wrong time! How successful you are is strongly influenced by the position of the Moon and the planets when you begin a particular activity. You could be more successful with the following activities if you start them on the days indicated.

Relationships

We all feel more empowered on some days than on others. This is because the planets have some power over us—their movement and their relationships to each other determine the ebb and flow of our energies. And our level of self-confidence and our sense of romantic magnetism play an important part in the way we behave in relationships.

Your daily planner tells you the ideal dates for meeting new friends, initiating a love affair, spending time with family and loved ones—it even tells you the most appropriate times for sexual encounters.

You'll be surprised at how much more impact you make in your relationships when you tune yourself in to the planetary energies on these special dates.

Falling in love/restoring love

During these times you could expect favourable energies to meet your soulmate or, if you've had difficulty in a relationship, to approach the one you love to rekindle both your and their emotional responses:

January	28, 30
February	25, 26
March	6, 7, 8, 28, 29, 30
April	25, 26, 30
May	1, 2, 5, 7, 26, 27, 28, 29

SCORPIO

June	2, 3, 23, 24, 26, 29, 30
July	22, 23, 26, 27
August	14, 15, 16, 17, 22, 23, 24
September	10, 14, 16, 19, 20, 21
October	9, 10, 11, 12, 13
November	25, 26
December	22, 23, 27, 31

Special times with friends and family

Socialising, partying and having a good time with those you enjoy being with is highly favourable under the following dates. These dates are excellent to spend time with family and loved ones in a domestic environment:

January	26
February	8, 12, 13, 14, 22, 23, 24
March	8, 22, 23
April	19, 27, 28
May	1, 2, 15, 16, 17, 24, 25, 28, 29
June	2, 3, 11, 12, 13, 22, 30
July	23, 26, 27
August	5, 6, 23, 24
September	16
October	13
November	8, 10, 24
December	19, 20, 21, 29

Healing or resuming relationships

If you're trying to get back together with the one you love and need a heart-to-heart or deep and meaningful, you can try the following dates to do so:

February	8, 12, 13, 14
March	8
April	18, 19
May	1, 2, 28, 29
June	2, 3, 30
July	23, 26, 27
August	23, 24
September	16
October	13
November	8
December	22, 23, 27

Sexual encounters

Physical and sexual energies are well favoured on the following dates. The energies of the planets enhance your moments of intimacy during these times:

January	5, 30
February	25, 26
March	6, 7, 8, 28, 29, 30
April	25, 26, 30
May	1, 2, 5, 7, 26, 27, 28, 29
June	2, 3, 23, 24, 26, 29, 30

SCORPIO

July	22, 23, 26, 27
August	23, 24
September	16
October	13
November	25, 26
December	22, 23, 27, 31

Health and wellbeing

Your aura and life force are susceptible to the movements of the planets; in particular, they respond to the phases of the Moon.

The following dates are the most appropriate times to begin a diet, have cosmetic surgery, or seek medical advice. They also tell you when the best times are to help others.

Feeling of wellbeing

Your physical as well as your mental alertness should be strong on these following dates. You can plan your activities and expect a good response from others:

January	8, 9, 26, 27
February	4, 5, 22, 23
March	31
April	18, 19, 27, 28
May	16, 17
June	21, 22
July	19
August	5, 6, 24, 25
September	12, 28, 30

October	8, 9
November	8, 10
December	19, 20, 21, 29, 30

Healing and medicine

This is good for approaching others who have expertise at a time when you need some deeper understanding. This is also favourable for any sort of healing or medication and making appointments with doctors or psychologists. Planning surgery around these dates should bring good results.

Often giving up our time and energy to assist others doesn't necessarily result in the expected outcome. By lending a helping hand to a friend on the following dates, the results should be favourable:

January	1, 20, 21, 22, 23, 24, 25, 26, 27, 28, 29, 30, 31
February	9, 10, 11, 12, 13, 14, 15, 16, 17, 18, 19, 20, 21, 22, 23, 24, 25, 26, 27, 28
March	2, 3, 4, 5, 6, 7, 8, 9, 22, 26, 28, 29, 30, 31
April	1, 10, 12, 15, 18, 20, 27, 28, 29, 30
May	1, 3, 7, 8, 9, 10, 11, 12
June	6, 7, 9, 13, 14, 15, 19, 21, 22
July	5, 6, 7, 8, 10, 12, 18, 19, 20, 25, 26
August	6, 7, 8, 9, 10, 29, 30, 31
September	1, 6, 27
October	8, 9, 10, 11, 12, 25, 26
November	18, 19, 20, 21, 22
December	10, 11, 12

Money

Money is an important part of life, and involves many decisions; decisions about borrowing, investing, spending. The ideal times for transactions are very much influenced by the planets, and whether your investment or nest egg grows or doesn't grow can often be linked to timing. Making your decisions on the following dates could give you a whole new perspective on your financial future.

Managing wealth and money

To build your nest egg, it's a good time to open your bank account and invest money on the following dates:

January	3, 4, 5, 10, 11, 16, 17, 23, 24, 25, 31
February	1, 6, 7, 12, 13, 14, 20, 21, 27, 28
March	5, 6, 7, 12, 13, 19, 26, 27
April	2, 3, 8, 9, 15, 17, 23, 24, 29, 30
May	5, 6, 7, 13, 14, 20, 21, 26, 27
June	2, 3, 9, 10, 16, 17, 18, 23, 24, 29, 30
July	6, 7, 8, 14, 15, 20, 21, 26, 27
August	2, 3, 4, 10, 11, 17, 18, 23, 24, 30, 31
September	6, 7, 13, 14, 19, 20, 26, 27
October	3, 4, 5, 10, 11, 16, 17, 18, 23, 24, 25, 31
November	1, 6, 7, 13, 14, 20, 21, 27, 28
December	4, 5, 10, 11, 17, 18, 24, 25, 26, 31

Spending

It's always fun to spend but the following dates are more in tune with this activity and are likely to give you better results:

2009: YOUR DAILY PLANNER

January	20, 28, 30
February	3
March	28, 29, 30
April	25, 26
May	31
June	1, 2, 7, 8, 9, 10, 28, 30
July	1, 2, 3, 26, 27, 29, 30
August	2, 3, 4, 5, 20, 21, 22, 23, 24, 25
September	19, 20, 21, 22, 23
October	9, 10
November	1, 7, 8, 17
December	27, 28

Selling

If you're thinking of selling something, whether it is small or large, consider the following dates as ideal times to do so:

January	3, 18, 19, 20, 21, 25, 26, 27, 28, 29, 30, 31
February	8, 10, 11, 12, 13, 14, 15, 18, 20, 22, 23, 24, 26, 28
March	2, 3, 4, 5, 6, 7, 8, 9, 16, 26, 27, 28, 31
April	5, 10, 19, 20, 23, 25, 27, 28, 29
May	1, 2, 7, 9, 13, 14, 21, 24, 25, 28, 29, 31
June	1, 2, 7, 8, 14, 16, 17, 20, 21, 22, 26, 30
July	1, 2, 3, 9, 10, 11, 15, 16, 17, 26, 27
August	2, 3, 4, 13, 14, 15, 16, 17
September	1, 2, 3, 4, 5, 6, 14, 15, 16, 17, 21, 22, 23, 24, 25, 26, 27, 28, 30, 31

SCORPIO

October	1, 2, 3, 4, 5, 6, 7, 8, 9, 10, 11, 12, 31
November	2, 3, 9, 10, 11, 12, 13, 25, 26, 27, 28, 29, 30
December	1, 2, 3, 7, 8, 9, 17, 20

Borrowing

Few of us like to borrow money, but if you must, taking out a loan on the following dates should be positive:

January	11, 18, 19, 20, 23, 24, 25
February	15, 16, 20, 21
March	14, 15, 19, 20
April	10, 11, 12, 15, 16, 17
May	9, 13, 14
June	9, 10
July	7, 8, 20, 21
August	17, 18
September	13, 14
October	10, 11
November	6, 7, 15, 16
December	4, 5, 12, 13, 14

Work and education

Your career is important to you, and continual improvement of your skills is therefore also crucial, professionally, mentally and socially. The dates below will help you find out the most appropriate times to improve your professional talents and commence new work or education associated with your work.

You may need to decide when to start learning a new skill, when to ask for a promotion, and even when to make an

2009: YOUR DAILY PLANNER

important career change. Here are the days when mental and educational power is strong.

Learning new skills

Educational pursuits are lucky and bring good results on the following dates:

January	8, 9
February	4, 5
March	3, 4, 10, 31
April	1, 6, 7, 27, 28
May	3, 4, 25, 30, 31
June	1, 6, 7, 27, 28
July	4, 5, 24, 25, 31
August	1, 21, 22, 27, 28, 29
September	23, 24, 25
October	21, 22
November	17, 18, 19
December	29, 30

Changing career path or profession

If you're feeling stuck and need to move into a new professional activity, changing jobs can be done at these times:

January	6, 7
February	2, 3
March	1, 2, 3, 4, 5, 6, 7, 8, 9, 10, 28, 29, 30
April	6, 7, 25, 26
May	3, 4, 30, 31
June	1, 27, 28

SCORPIO

July	6, 24, 25
August	2, 3, 4, 21, 22, 30, 31
September	26, 27
October	23, 24, 25
November	2, 20, 21, 29, 30
December	1, 17, 18, 27, 28

Promotion, professional focus and hard work

To increase your mental focus and achieve good results from the work you do, promotions are likely on these dates that follow:

January	4, 5, 6, 11, 12, 13, 14, 15, 16, 21
February	6
March	18, 19, 20
April	8, 28, 29
May	12, 21
June	25, 26
July	1, 2, 3, 8, 15, 17
August	4, 14, 15, 16, 17, 18, 22, 23, 24
September	14, 15, 18, 19, 23, 24, 25, 26
October	22
November	7, 10, 11, 12, 17
December	1, 2, 3, 7, 28

Travel

Setting out on a holiday or adventurous journey is exciting. To gain the most out of your holidays and journeys, travelling on the following dates is likely to give you a sense of fulfilment:

2009: YOUR DAILY PLANNER

January	9, 10, 28, 29, 30, 31
February	1, 4, 5, 26
March	3, 4, 5, 6, 7, 27, 31
April	27, 28, 29
May	1, 2, 25
June	6, 7, 25, 26
July	6, 31
August	1, 2, 21, 22, 23, 24, 29
September	19, 20, 23, 24, 25, 26, 27
October	1, 2, 3, 25, 28, 29, 30, 31
November	1, 17, 18, 26, 28
December	17, 18, 23, 26

Beauty and grooming

Believe it or not, cutting your hair or nails has a powerful effect on your body's electromagnetic energy. If you cut your hair or nails at the wrong time of the month, you can reduce your level of vitality significantly. Use these dates to ensure you optimise your energy levels by staying in tune with the stars.

Hair and nails

January	1, 2, 8, 9, 21, 22, 28, 29, 30
February	4, 5, 17, 18, 19, 25, 26
March	3, 4, 16, 17, 18, 24, 25, 31
April	1, 13, 14, 20, 21, 22, 27, 28, 29, 30
May	8, 10, 11, 12, 18, 19, 24, 25
June	6, 7, 8, 14, 15, 21, 22

SCORPIO

July	4, 5, 11, 12, 13, 18, 19, 31
August	1, 7, 8, 9, 14, 15, 16, 27, 28, 29
September	4, 5, 11, 12, 23, 24, 25
October	1, 2, 8, 9, 21, 22, 28, 29, 30
November	4, 5, 17, 18, 19, 25, 26
December	2, 3, 15, 16, 22, 23, 29, 30

Therapies, massage and self-pampering

January	18, 19, 20, 26, 27
February	3, 6, 7, 8, 12, 13, 14, 15, 16, 22, 23, 24
March	6, 8, 28, 29, 30
April	5, 8, 9, 18, 19, 25, 26, 29, 30
May	1, 2, 5, 7, 9, 15, 16, 17, 22, 23, 26, 27, 28, 29
June	2, 3, 4, 5, 11, 12, 13, 19, 20, 23, 24, 26, 30
July	1, 2, 3, 9, 10, 23, 26, 27, 28, 29, 30
August	6, 12, 13, 17, 18, 19, 20, 23, 24, 25, 26
September	1, 2, 13, 14, 16
October	10, 11, 12, 13, 16, 17, 27
November	8, 9, 10, 13, 16, 23, 24, 29, 30
December	1, 4, 5, 6, 7, 10, 11, 12, 13, 14, 19, 20, 21, 27, 28, 31

MILLS & BOON
MODERN™

...International affairs, seduction and passion guaranteed

The Greek Tycoon's Pregnant Wife
Anne Mather

Miranda Lee
Blackmailed into the Italian's Bed

MILLS & BOON
MODERN™

8 brand-new titles each month

Available on the first Friday of every month
from WHSmith, ASDA, Tesco
and all good bookshops
www.millsandboon.co.uk

GEN/01/RTL11

MILLS & BOON
MODERN
Heat

If you like Mills & Boon Modern you'll love Modern Heat!

Strong, sexy alpha heroes, sizzling storylines and exotic locations from around the world – what more could you want!

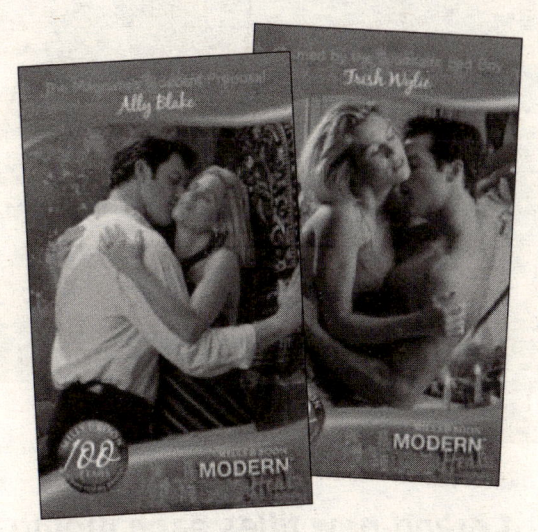

2 brand-new titles each month

Available on the first Friday of every month
from WHSmith, ASDA, Tesco
and all good bookshops
www.millsandboon.co.uk

MILLS & BOON
Romance

Pure romance, pure emotion

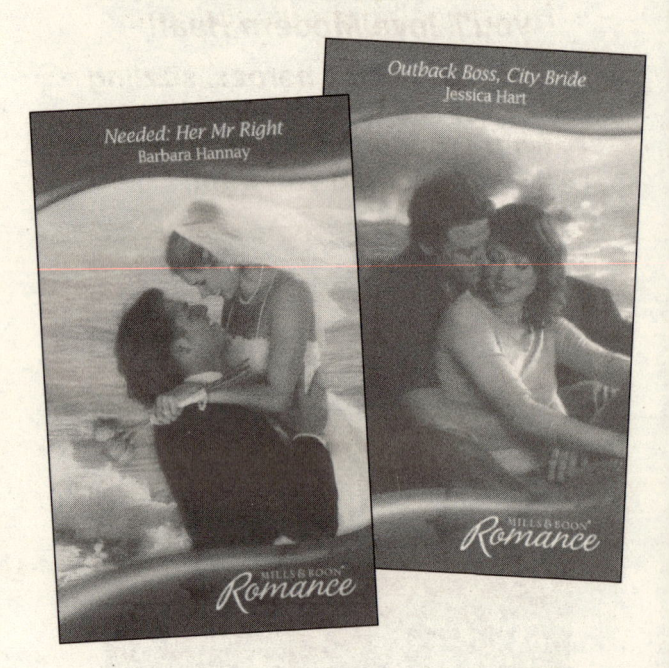

Needed: Her Mr Right
Barbara Hannay

Outback Boss, City Bride
Jessica Hart

4 brand-new titles each month

Available on the first Friday of every month
from WHSmith, ASDA, Tesco
and all good bookshops
www.millsandboon.co.uk

GEN/02/RTL11

MILLS & BOON
MEDICAL™

Pulse-raising romance – Heart-racing medical drama

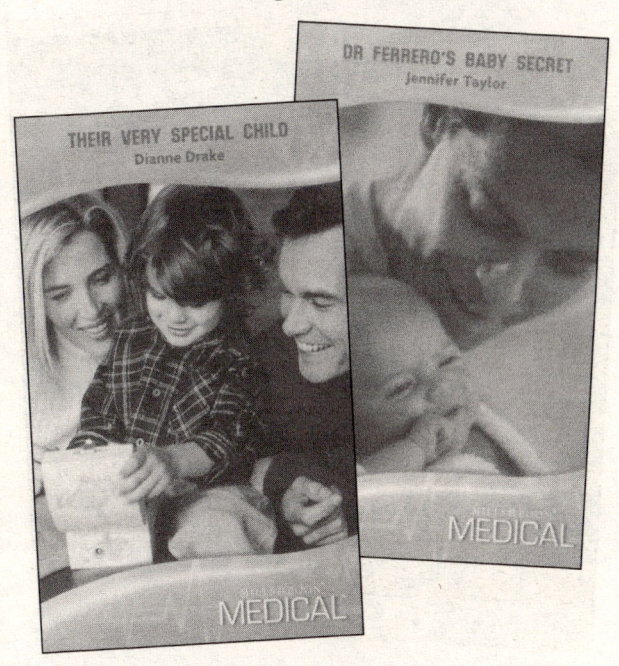

6 brand-new titles each month

Available on the first Friday of every month
from WHSmith, ASDA, Tesco
and all good bookshops
www.millsandboon.co.uk

GEN/03/RTL11

MILLS & BOON
Historical

Rich, vivid and passionate

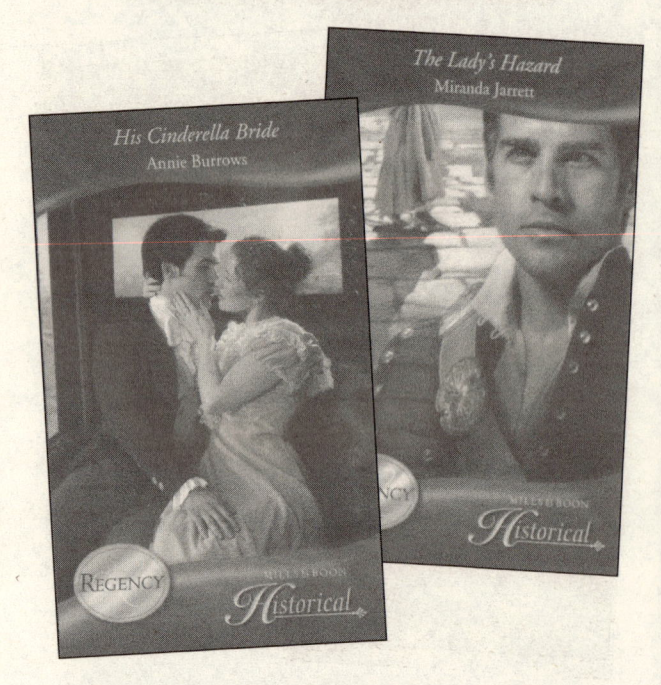

His Cinderella Bride
Annie Burrows

The Lady's Hazard
Miranda Jarrett

4 brand-new titles each month

Available on the first Friday of every month
from WHSmith, ASDA, Tesco
and all good bookshops
www.millsandboon.co.uk

GEN/04/RTL11

MILLS & BOON
Blaze

Scorching hot sexy reads...

GOING ALL THE WAY
Isabel Sharpe

HIDDEN OBSESSION
Joanne Rock

4 brand-new titles each month

Available on the first Friday of every month
from WHSmith, ASDA, Tesco
and all good bookshops
www.millsandboon.co.uk

GEN/14/RTL11

MILLS & BOON
Special Edition

Life, love and family

6 brand-new titles each month

Available on the third Friday of every month
from WHSmith, ASDA, Tesco
and all good bookshops
www.millsandboon.co.uk

GEN/23/RTL11

MILLS & BOON
*Super*ROMANCE

Enjoy the drama, explore the emotions, experience the relationships

4 brand-new titles each month

Available on the third Friday of every month
from WHSmith, ASDA, Tesco
and all good bookshops
www.millsandboon.co.uk

GEN/38/RTL11

MILLS & BOON

INTRIGUE

Breathtaking romance & adventure

8 brand-new titles each month

Available on the third Friday of every month
from WHSmith, ASDA, Tesco
and all good bookshops
www.millsandboon.co.uk

GEN/46/RTL11

MILLS & BOON
Desire 2-in-1

2 passionate, dramatic love stories in each book

3 brand-new titles to choose from each month

Available on the third Friday of every month
from WHSmith, ASDA, Tesco
and all good bookshops
www.millsandboon.co.uk

GEN/51/RTL11

Celebrate our centenary year with 24 special short stories!

ONLY £1.49! EACH

A special 100th Birthday Collection from your favourite authors including:

Penny Jordan • Diana Palmer • Lucy Gordon
Carole Mortimer • Betty Neels
Debbie Macomber • Sharon Kendrick
Alexandra Sellers • Nicola Cornick

Two stories published every month from January 2008 to January 2009

Collect all 24 stories to complete the set!

MILLS & BOON
Pure reading pleasure

www.millsandboon.co.uk